MW01102059

MOVIES and
The Battle of The Sexes

MOVIES and
The Battle of the Sexes

By

ZetMec

The GOOD MOVIE GUIDE Series

Copyright © 2012

by ZetMec Productions

All rights reserved, including the right to reproduce this work in
any form whatsoever, without permission in writing
from the publisher, except for brief passages in connection with
a review.

Cover design by ZetMec Productions,
www.moviesandthebattleofthesexes.com
in conjunction with Shelley's Graphic Arts
and Illumination Graphics, www.illuminationgraphics.com

Cover art copyright © 2010
All rights reserved

Virtualbookworm.com Publishing Inc.
www.virtualbookworm.com

Printed in the United States of America

To order this book visit www.virtualbookworm.com

ISBN -13: 978-0-9816204-1-1   ISBN -10: 0-9816204-1-8

DEDICATION

To all my favorite Movie Lovers:

To the writers, directors, producers, editors, cinematographers, visionaries, casts & crews, and anyone who ever helped a good story come to fruition up there on the Silver Screen.

To Leonard Maltin, one of the all-time greatest Movie Lovers, who once said, "the daily dance between the sexes never gets old…."

To Kate Hepburn who created on screen the perfectly imperfect image of a modern, independent woman, because she was herself, in truth, a genuinely modern and independent woman. "Marriage is a series of desperate arguments people feel passionately about." --- Kate Hepburn

And, of course, to Mom & Dad...thanks for all the really swell times and all those terrific movies. Love you forever.

CONTENTS

ACKNOWLEDGMENTS

TCM – The movie channel that has it all—style plus great movies, interviews and entertainment. Also, thanks for the *Forbidden Hollywood Collection*, Vol. 1, 2 & 3 [DVDs].

imdb.com – The most extensive online source of movie info.

Netflix – The biggest source of rentable movies ever!

brainyquote.com – Great source of entertainment quotes.

VideoHound's Golden Movie Retriever, 2001 – A wealth of info all in one book! [I have a newer one, but this one's annotated!]

Bobby Riggs & Billie Jean King – The Battle of the Sexes tennis match took place September 20, 1973 in Houston, TX, furthering the ongoing cause of women's struggle for equality.

D.J.'s Video – The best video store in the Rogue Valley, and a great source of cinema-related books and materials.

Deborah Hopping, www.illuminationgraphics.com – Book cover designer, great communicator, and skilled advisor.

Über Geek (Ethan Knowles), www.geek2d.com – Website builder [www.moviesandthemeaningoflife.com], and adept problem solver.

Dan Ragen – Cadie's dad and the guy who inspired the "Great Conquering Hero" movie list.

Marla Estes, M.A. – Movie Lover, educator and big believer in The School of the Examined Life [www.marlaestes.com].

Lloyd M. Haines – Ginger and Shasta's dad, Founder of SANCTUARY ONE [www.sanctuaryone.org], and the guy who supported my investment in some really good marketing info.

Emmalisa Whalley [www.watermarksoftheworld.com] – Webmaster [www.zetmec.com], entrepreneur, and trusted advisor.

Shelley Carpenter, Shelley's Graphic Arts – Life-long advisor, designer, and artist *extraordinaire*.

Van La Master – Old friend and contributor of the best battle-of-the-sexes advice known to either side, "Relax!"

Ann Hodge – Fellow Movie Lover, great friend & patron, and first-class listening post for book and movie ideas.

"Bubba and the Nordski," AKA Bert & Janet Davis – Movie Lovers and loyal friends, battling together successfully now for 27 years.

Harry Wolfe – March 19, 1948 - June 14, 2012. The guy who talked me into becoming an ordained minister, then talked me into marrying him to Cheryl. Only Harry!

My Reluctant Moviegoer – Friend, editor, faithful advisor and Neo's dad.

Thank you one and all!

FOREWORD

Sexual politics has been standard operating procedure for humans since Adam and Eve. And although we can't be sure who corrupted whom back in Eden, we all know full well conflict is still a fundamental part of gender consciousness. It's also true that the battle of the sexes... apparently a deep-seated part of our nature... has always been reliable fodder for early motion pictures, and in every film decade since.

And even though every era of the 20th Century produced its own gender issues, movies of a specific decade don't necessarily reflect traditional thinking of that era. Some silent films, for example, are very modern in their depiction of the sexes, while newer movies can be total throwbacks to a more lop-sided, weaker-sex machismo. Consequently, this guide will have old movies on the "21st Century" movie list, as well as movies from the 2000s on lists from earlier decades.

Old or new, however, films listed in *Movies and The Battle of the Sexes* always address gender issues in an edgy fashion, saving the more romantic, true-love stuff for another day. These are the kind of movies where men and women always get into some nice, juicy little scrap somewhere along the way. Sometimes it's just a difference of opinion before falling into each other's arms, and sometimes it's a fight to the death; but, by gum, it's a stronger brew than the usual swill. So, kick back, pick a DVD to your liking, and have a cocktail. You'll feel better soon!

The Lists Legend

The seven sections of this guide represent seven sub-genres (see "Lists" below) of Battle of The Sexes movies. Short summaries of these Battle of The Sexes movies, and a few longer summaries, appear on the right-hand side of the book, along with Buzzometer (Buzz = backstory & trivia) and Vizometer (Viz = visuals & music) listings.

On the left-hand side of the book, you'll find many favorite movie-related gender-consciousness quotes. On the left you'll also find classic cocktail recipes for drinks served in some of the Battle of The Sexes movies listed in this book, and a few new 21st Century cocktails as well.

Battle-of-The-Sexes Movie Lists

- It's a Man's World
- Sex, Drugs & Red Hot Jazz
- The Kate Hepburn Model
- Love Is a Battlefield*
- Girls Just Want to Have Fun**
- The Great Conquering Hero
- Sexual Warfare in the 21st Century

*   With thanks to the mighty Pat Benatar.

**   With thanks to the magnificent Cyndi Lauper.

"No lady's dangerous if
you know how
to handle her."

— Cab driver, *Women on the Verge of a
Nervous Breakdown*

LIST I – It's a Man's World

"A swell start you gave me. ... Nothing but men!
Dirty, rotten men!"
— Barbara Stanwyck to her father,
Baby Face

Top "It's a Man's World" Movies

* *Male and Female, 1919*

* *Don Juan, 1926*

* *Battle of the Sexes, 1928*

* *The Champ, 1931*

* *King Kong, 1933*

* *The King and I, 1956*

* *Pretty Woman, 1990*

"She cooks as good as she looks, Ted."

— Walter Eberhart,
The Stepford Wives (1975)

It's a Man's World MOVIE LIST

1. **Tillie's Punctured Romance,** 1914 (Silent).
Mack Sennett film pits Charlie Chaplin, gigolo, and
girlfriend Mabel Normand against Marie Dressler, the
farmer's zaftig daughter.

2. **The Perils of Pauline,** 1914. (Silent, Serial)
Pearl White.   Damsel in distress is menaced by the
villain and, among other things, tied to the railroad
tracks…or is she?

3. **Male and Female,** 1919 (Silent). Gloria
Swanson. Cecil B. DeMille looks at social-standing
roles as well as gender status.

4. **Broken Blossoms,** 1919 (Silent). D. W. Griffith's
tragedy stars Lillian Gish as a frail waif abused by her
father and (nearly) rescued by an unusual male
friendship.

5. **The Mark of Zorro,** 1920 (Silent). Douglas
Fairbanks. The dim-witted woman in Zorro's life needs
a lot of rescuing.

6. **The Affairs of Anatol,** 1921 (Silent). Wallace
Reid & Gloria Swanson. Married man decides to
rescue needy women other than his wife.

7. **Foolish Wives,** 1922 (Silent). Erich von Stroheim's
eccentric Don Juan seduces women, conning them out
of their money…until he gets his just desserts.

8. **Don Juan,** 1926 (Silent). John Barrymore & hosts
of others. All women are putty in his hands.

9. **Sunrise: A Song of Two Humans,** 1927
(Silent). F.W. Murnau's moving portrayal of a
bewitched husband torn between rescuing his loving
wife and running off with a wicked city woman.

"I need love...and women need men to feel complete."

— Amy,
Amy's O

10. **The Battle of the Sexes,** 1928 (Silent), (also, 1914 and 1959). Golddigger seduces family man. **QUOTE:** (Opening Dialogue Card) "The battle of the sexes – always being fought and never being won."

11. **The Love Parade**, 1929. Jeannette MacDonald and Maurice Chevalier star in this Ernst Lubitsch musical comedy about an emissary who marries a Queen but resents having to play second fiddle to the woman he takes orders from. Best Picture nominee.

12. A Free Soul, 1931. Norma Shearer gets caught up in one man's wicked web and has to be rescued by two other men in her life.

13. **The Champ,** 1931. Wallace Beery & Jackie Cooper. It's really a man's world in this father-and-son-bonding melodrama—mom just picks up the pieces.

14. Call Her Savage, 1932. Naughty Clara Bow.

15. Tarzan the Ape Man, 1932. The first Tarzan & Jane for Johnny Weissmuller & Maureen O'Sullivan.

16. Female, 1933. Tough-minded business woman tries to love-'em and leave-'em, like a man.

17. Queen Christina, 1933. Greta Garbo dresses as a man to escape the restrictions and vulnerabilities of being 1600s female Swedish royalty.

18. **King Kong,** 1933 (Also, 1976 and 2005). Fay Wray (Also, Jessica Lange and Naomi Watts). It's a man's world even during the Depression. What's a girl to do? Starve, or get mixed up with some big ape?!

19. Captain Blood, 1935. Errol Flynn & Olivia de Havilland. Doctor, slave, swashbuckler, woman tamer…in like Flynn!

20. Sex Madness, 1938. Sex ALWAYS leads to syphilis…or something bad!

"First of all, Rat, you never let on how much you like a girl…Two, you always call the shots."

— Mike Damone,
Fast Times at Ridgemont High

21. **Pride and Prejudice**, 1940, 1995 (BBC), and 2005's *Pride & Prejudice.* Both the magnificent Lizzie and the lovely Mr. Darcy suffer from living lives of restriction and restraint in a mostly man's world.

22. **Mildred Pierce**, 1945. Joan Crawford. Victimized by weak men, and then by her uppity daughter too.

23. **Undercurrent**, 1946. Kate Hepburn, Robert Taylor & Robert Mitchum. On the verge of becoming a spinster scientist, Ann Hamilton marries a hot-blooded man and becomes the target of his abuse.

24. **Notorious**, 1946. Playgirl, Ingrid Bergman, has to pay for the sins of her father, and is dominated by two men on either side of the evil axis. Cary Grant rescues her from Nazi Claude Rains just in the nick.

25. **Gilda**, 1946. Rita Hayworth & Glenn Ford. Who can forget Gilda's no-strip striptease? **VIZ**: Songs, "Amado Mio" (covered by Pink Martini on their *Sympathique* album) and "Put the Blame on Mame." **QUOTE:** "If I'd been a ranch, they would've named me 'The Bar Nothing'." — Gilda

26. **The Red Shoes**, 1948. Michael Powell and Emeric Pressburger's great film about one dancer's tragic loyalty to a powerful and controlling man.

27. **The King and I**, 1956. Yul Brynner & Deborah Kerr. She's unworthy in the King's eyes as a Christian AND as a woman. "Et cetera, et cetera, et cetera!" — The King

28. **Funny Face**, 1957. Stanley Donen's film about a beautiful shop girl (Audrey Hepburn) manipulated by a photographer (Fred Astaire) and the whims of fashion.

29. **Goldfinger**, 1964. Sean Connery. The gilded girl dies and the smart chick is named "Pussy Galore."

"I don't mind living in a man's world as long as I can be a woman in it."

— Marilyn Monroe

30. **Alfie,** 1966. Michael Caine. Alfie's wickedly callous sex life is the only "real" life, as far as he's concerned.

31. **Young Frankenstein,** 1974. Gene Wilder, Teri Garr, Peter Boyle, Cloris Leachman & Marty Feldman. Mel Brooks classic where the boys are in charge. **VIZ:** You gotta check out Peter Boyle and Gene Wilder doing their rendition of "Puttin' on the Ritz." **QUOTE:** Dr. Frederick Frankenstein (standing in front of the huge castle doors), "What knockers!" Inga: "Oh, thank you doctor!"

32. **Alice,** 1990. Mia Farrow is dominated by her husband, her boyfriend, a Chinese healer and a ghost in Woody Allen's poor-little-rich-and-neurotic-girl saga.

33. **Pretty Woman,** 1990. Julia Roberts plays a hooker with a heart of gold rescued from her hard-knock life by Richard Gere, the handsome rich guy.

34. **Moulin Rouge!,** 2001. Nicole Kidman & Ewan McGregor. Poor little Satine, the consumptive courtesan, and Christian, her poet lover, subject to the whims of rich men in a man's world.

"A man is the necessary evil, the necessary evil is he..."

(Song, "A Man Is a Necessary Evil")

— Virginia Mayo, *Painting the Clouds*

Pretty Woman

There are a lot of contentious male-female relationships in this movie, as alluded to by the two girls, Vivian & Kit (Julia Roberts & Laura San Giacomo), who deal with horny, disrespectful johns on a daily basis. It's caused them to be cynical and develop rules about what they will and will not do, which seems only natural. The fact, however, that both girls are very smart and strikingly beautiful doesn't seem that natural, but, hey... it's a fairytale about star-crossed hookers, not a documentary.

If it were a documentary, *Pretty Woman* might have explored that strange, counterintuitive lack of respect men have for ladies of the evening who provide those services men have always needed through the centuries—sex on demand. And if that weren't demeaning enough, the pimps controlling and turning out young prostitutes are even worse—virtual sex slavers. But again, this is a Cinderella story and everything that can go right, does, which makes it the perfect battle-of-the-sexes fantasy as envisioned by its director, Garry Marshall.

Vivian's beautiful, her savior (Richard Gere) is handsome; she's smart and funny, he's experienced and rich. At first, they circle each other cautiously, and although appropriately suspicious, fall in love anyway. There's a moment or two of adversity and a bit of a learning curve along the way that amps up sexual tension, but in the end, the gorgeous hooker with a heart of gold is rescued by the handsome prince who has both their best interests at heart. End of battle, beginning of Happily-Ever-After. In a man's world, who could ask for anything more?

"You dominate me! You overwhelm me!"

— Ginger Rogers,
Oh, Men! Oh, Women!

BUZZ: There are lots of movie references in *Pretty Woman*, like when she says "let's watch old movies…" or the narrator says, "Welcome to Hollywood!" There's also a specific one Edward makes to *West Side Story*, and, of course, there's a very obvious reference to *Cinderella* by Vivian ("I want the fairy tale."), as well as a more profane version of that by Kit.

VIZ: No matter what you think of her role in *Pretty Woman*, Julia Roberts is luminous in the part. She was nominated for Best Actress playing Vivian.

"You aren't too smart, are you? I like that in a man."

— Kathleen Turner,
Body Heat

LIST II – Sex, Drugs & Red Hot Jazz
[mostly pre-code]

"Sex is God's joke on human beings."
— Bette Davis

Top "Sex, Drugs & Red Hot Jazz" Movies

* *Pandora's Box, 1929*

* *The Divorcee, 1930*

* *Red-Headed Woman, 1932*

* *Baby Face, 1933*

* *I'm No Angel, 1933*

* *Flying Down to Rio, 1933*

* *Tarzan and His Mate, 1934*

"Give a man a free hand and he'll run it all over you."

— Mae West

Sex, Drugs & Red Hot Jazz MOVIE LIST

1. **Easy Virtue,** 1928 (Silent). Early Hitchcock about a woman's scandalous past.

2. **The Patsy,** 1928 (Silent). King Vidor's modern Cinderella story with plucky Marion Davies who must save herself when no one else will.

3. **Pandora's Box,** 1929, German (Silent). Louise Brooks plays the amazing Lulu, a free spirit who's spreading her wings as a sexually-liberated female, and fast becoming the source from which all the troubles of the world spill out.

4. **The Single Standard,** 1929 (Silent). Greta Garbo tries to prove to an attractive painter she's capable of the same free-spirited "Philosophy of Love" (a book she emulates) as men.

5. **Their Own Desire,** 1929. Early talkie where man/woman, husband/wife issues run rampant.

6. **The Divorcee,** 1930. **BUZZ:** With some very provocative photos, Norma Shearer shocked hubby Irving Thalberg, MGM's "Prince of Hollywood," into believing she could play the sexy role of Jerry in *The Divorcee*. She won Best Actress for her trouble.

7. **Strangers May Kiss,** 1931. Free-thinking modern woman doesn't believe in marriage—until she discovers her lover already has a wife and another life.

8. **Other Men's Women,** 1931. Mary Astor & Joan Blondell. **QUOTE:** "Listen, baby, I'm A.P.O. ... Ain't Puttin' Out!" — Marie

9. **Safe in Hell,** 1931. A good girl, once gone bad, tries to remain true to one man, but is persecuted by the men she refuses sexual favors.

"Sex: the thing that takes up the least amount of time and causes the most amount of trouble."

— John Barrymore

10. **Private Lives**, 1931. Norma Shearer & Robert Montgomery, now divorced, meet again at a hotel where both are on honeymoons with someone new. A very funny Nöel Coward love-hate relationship. **QUOTE:** "Certain women should be struck regularly, like gongs." — Elyot

11. **The Smiling Lieutenant**, 1931. Claudette Colbert teaches her boyfriend's wife how to win over the guy in sexually charged Lubitsch musical.

12. **Platinum Blonde**, 1931. Loretta Young & Jean Harlow in an early Capra. Rich and beautiful socialite turns her reporter husband into a lap dog.

13. **Blonde Crazy**, 1931. Joan Blondell & James Cagney are Depression-era con artists.

14. **The Maltese Falcon**, 1931. Pre-Bogie version of the black-falcon treasure hunt is cheekier and snappier with a smarter, more sinful woman. [Also see *Satan Met a Lady*, 1936]

15. **Kept Husbands**, 1931. Joel McCrea. Modern woman/spoiled rich girl "bags" her man.

16. **Hot Saturday**, 1932. Cary Grant understands what a woman needs.

17. **Red-Headed Woman,** 1932. Jean Harlow is a loose woman and an amoral homewrecker.

18. **Vanity Fair**, 1932 (AKA *Indecent*). Becky Sharp (Myrna Loy), with calculated guile, claws her way to the top. [Also see *Becky Sharp*, 1935]

19. **Red Dust**, 1932. Jean Harlow, Clark Gable & Mary Astor. Nothing like a little gender tussle in the jungle.

20. **Trouble in Paradise**, 1932. Miriam Hopkins & Herbert Marshall. Two married cons are equally good at what they do, and they do it together very well.

"Men are creatures with two legs and eight hands."

— Jayne Mansfield

21. **Faithless**, 1932. A spoiled heiress loses everything and is forced to live at the whim of men. **QUOTE:** "I don't believe in delinquent girls—silly weaklings." — Carol (Tallulah Bankhead)

22. **Shanghai Express**, 1932. This train carries a "cargo of sin" (women) and bad reputations.

23. **Grand Hotel**, 1932. Greta Garbo, Joan Crawford, John & Lionel Barrymore live out tense and secret love lives at Berlin's ritziest hotel.

24. **Love Is a Racket**, 1932. Mary is more interested in her career than in her boyfriend, Jimmy, a hopeless romantic.

25. **Dinner at Eight**, 1933. Cukor's wonderfully witty women spar with each other and the men in their lives. **QUOTE:** "I'm going to be a lady if it kills me!" — Kitty (Jean Harlow)

26. **Baby Face,** 1933. Barbara Stanwyck is a man hater, but sleeps her way to the top with gusto.

27. **Ann Carver's Profession**, 1933. Fay Wray is a wife and a lawyer who succeeds mightily, even as her husband (Gene Raymond) fails to keep up.

28. **Torch Singer**, 1933. Sally (Claudette Colbert) failed as a wife and mother, so now she sings sad songs until she can fulfill her greatest desire.

29. **Mystery of the Wax Museum**, 1933. Feisty girl reporter saves the day, bests the boys and still has fun! Pre-*Casablanca* Michael Curtiz vehicle.

30. **The Story of Temple Drake**, 1933. Forced sex (pre-code) and the Stockholm Syndrome make this film controversial to this day.

"Friendship's much more lasting than love." — Mildred (Joan Crawford)

"Yeah, but it isn't as entertaining."
— Wally (Jack Carson), *Mildred Pierce*

Baby Face

Barbara Stanwyck, George Brent and a host of others (including a bit player named John Wayne) star in this pre-code cutie about a wicked little number named Lily Powers who's literally choking to death on dirty old men in a sooty little factory town. When Lily's vile father blows himself up in a still accident (hooch), another father-figure acts as her mentor and tries to get her to take control of her own life. "Don't let people mislead you. You must be a master, not a slave. Be clean, be strong, defiant...and you will be a success. Leave this horrible town, for god's sake!" And when you see the look on Lily's face, you know she's gonna do it.

Even though she's smart and brave and savvy, Lily's been putting her dad's base desires ahead of her own...but no more! She hops a freight car with her friend and maid, Chico, and they hit the streets of NYC where Lily wheedles her way into a job at a bank, then a promotion, in no time at all. Soon she's sleeping with anyone that can get her one more rung higher up the ladder. And by the time she reaches the top, she's accrued a tidy sum of cash, jewels and hearts. Then something strange comes over her—this golddigger, this wanton woman has somehow acquired a conscience along the way.

Buzz: As Lily's financial worth goes up, her gowns by Orry-Kelly get more and more stunning.

VIZ: One of the primary tunes (W.C. Handy's "St. Louis Blues," 1914) is an instrumental number—a bluesy and melancholy mark of the Jazz Age.

Martini

INGREDIENTS

Taken from the side of a 1930s cocktail shaker:

2 parts gin
1 part dry vermouth
1/2 part sweet vermouth
1 dash Angostura Bitters

PROCEDURE

Martinis were much sweeter and had more flavor in the early 1900s than they do now, which during Prohibition helped cover up bad booze. They were shaken with ice and served in small, stemmed cocktail glasses, no olive.

Since the 40s, Martinis dropped sweet vermouth and bitters altogether as gin became more refined, and drastically decreased the amount of dry vermouth as well. They also added olives and began stirring Martinis instead of shaking them so as to retain the liquid's clarity.

There are Wet Martinis, Dry Martinis, Perfect Martinis, and Dirty (olive brine) Martinis; stirred Martinis that don't bruise the gin, the colder "shaken not stirred" variety, and vodka Martinis, all served with either olives or lemon peel in a slant-sided glass. Pick your poison and bottoms up!

COCKTAIL FEATURED in *The Thin Man, All About Eve* and *The Lady Eve*

31. **Penthouse**, 1933. Myrna Loy. **QUOTE:** Jack: "Oh, I've been stupid, very stupid." Gertie: "Of course. You're a man."

32. **I'm No Angel,** 1933. Mae West was one of the biggest reasons for enforcement of the Hays Code. **QUOTE:** "It's not the men in your life that counts, it's the life in your men." — Tira

33. **When Ladies Meet**, 1933. Ann Harding & Robert Montgomery. The philosophy of husband stealing.

34. **Flying Down to Rio,** 1933. Where Fred & Ginger's foreheads meet and hips sway to the Carioca, and chorus girls dance on the wings of airplanes.

35. **Gold Diggers of 1933**, 1933. Ruby Keeler, Ginger Rogers, Joan Blondell & Dick Powell. The girls have to stick together because it's the Depression, but many of their individual charms are on display. **VIZ:** Song, "We're in the Money!"

36. **The Thin Man**, 1934. William Powell & Myrna Loy. Nick & Nora go head-to-head and martini-to-martini in both marriage and murder.

37. **Tarzan and His Mate,** 1934. Jane engages in a little nude swimming with Tarzan. "The best weapon a woman has is a man's imagination." — Jane

38. **This Man Is Mine**, 1934. Irene Dunne & Ralph Bellamy. Toni and Jim are having a little disagreement about Jim hooking up with his ex-fiancé.

39. **The Scarlet Empress**, 1934. Marlene Dietrich plays a headstrong German princess who outwits the men around her to become Catherine the Great of Russia.

40. **Riptide**, 1934. Norma Shearer tries valiantly to resist temptation (Robert Montgomery)…sort of.

[After Junior asks Sugar about her gig with *Sweet Sue and Her Society Syncopators*:]

**"Syncopators. Does that mean you play that very fast music…jazz?" — He
"Yeah. Real hot." — She
"I guess some like it hot. I personally prefer classical music." — He**

— Tony Curtis & Marilyn Monroe, *Some Like It Hot*

I'm No Angel

Mae West supposedly single-handedly saved Paramount Pictures from impending bankruptcy with *She Done Him Wrong*. In gratitude, mogul Adolph Zukor promised Mae she could do anything she wanted for her next film, and this—what is arguably considered her best film—is the result. She packed this movie with her own personal brand of sex appeal; with the lovely Cary Grant; with a hilarious courtroom scene where she's got the judge and jury eating out of her hand; and, some of the best one-liner double entendres you've ever heard.

Tira (Mae) ALWAYS has something slightly bawdy to say, like: "When I'm good, I'm very good. But, when I'm bad... [winks] I'm better." Or, remember "Beulah, peel me a grape"? Yep, that's in this movie, as well as "Never let one man worry your mind. Find 'em, fool 'em and forget 'em!" There are many more, in addition to these two great taglines for the film: "Come up and see me sometime—any time!" She doesn't say it exactly like that to Cary in this one, but it's one of Mae's classic lines. And my favorite summary tagline for *I'm No Angel*: "A story about a gal who lost her reputation—and never missed it!"

But the thing is, as much as Mae may have saved Paramount Pictures from demise, this smart, funny and naughty little movie may have also been single-handedly responsible for more rigorous enforcement by the Hays Code in censuring good pre-code material by grinding it down to less "dire" fare. The censors went a little nuts, in fact, when they heard some of Mae's lyrics for songs in this movie, and it only got approved after they were much toned down. One of the big changes was song title, "Nobody Does It Like a Dallas Man" which had to be reinvented as "Nobody Loves Me Like a Dallas Man." Anyway, the Hays Office never ever approved the film for re-release.

"Women and men, unfortunately, are just not the same. They're not the same."

— Katharine Hepburn

Dick Cavett Show (aired Sept 14, 1973)

LIST III – The Kate Hepburn Model

"I never realized until lately that women were supposed to be the inferior sex."
— Katharine Hepburn

Top "The Kate Hepburn Model" Movies

* *Little Women, 1933*

* *The Philadelphia Story, 1940*

* *Woman of the Year, 1942*

* *Adam's Rib, 1949*

* *The African Queen, 1951*

* *Pat and Mike, 1952*

* *The Lion in Winter, 1968*

"Trying to be fascinating is an asinine position to be in."

— Katharine Hepburn

The Kate Hepburn Model MOVIE LIST

1. **Little Women,** 1933. Louisa May Alcott's story of four very different sisters. Jo curses ("Christopher Columbus!") and just doesn't know how to be ladylike.

2. **Christopher Strong,** 1933. Directed by Dorothy Arzner, Kate's controversial role of a daring aviatrix challenges a woman's "place," yet, in the end, holds to old gender clichés.

3. **Sylvia Scarlett,** 1935. Kate masquerades as "Sylvester" in a strange con-artist gender-bender film, her first with Cary Grant.

4. **A Woman Rebels,** 1936. As the daughter of a suffragette in real life, Kate plays a headstrong and tenacious Victorian woman fighting for women's rights.

5. **The Philadelphia Story,** 1940. From a well-to-do Philadelphia family, the nearly perfect taskmaster, Tracy Lord (Kate), rebels against a lot of bad male behavior in her life. **BUZZ:** Although this was Kate's last pairing—and one of the best—with Cary Grant, it was Jimmy Stewart who won the Oscar. **QUOTE:** George: [to his horse] "What's the matter, Bessie? You seem worried." Dinah: "Maybe that's because his name is Jack."

6. **Woman of the Year,** 1942. Kate's first film with Spencer Tracy won Best Original Screenplay. Tess and Sam are married, but Tess, a strong, independent woman, doesn't really "get" the importance of treating their relationship with respect.

7. **Without Love,** 1945. There's lot of snappy dialogue between Hepburn and Tracy who've committed to a working partnership and a marriage of convenience, only to have it take on a deeper meaning.

Sazerac

INGREDIENTS

1 sugar cube
2 ounces Rye Whiskey
1/2 tsp absinthe or Herbsaint
4 dashes Peychaud's Bitters
lemon peel

PROCEDURE

Fill an old-fashioned glass with ice.

In a second glass, saturate the sugar cube with Peychaud's bitters, then crush it. Add rye to the second glass containing the sugar and bitters and stir gently with an ice cube or two to chill it.

Empty the ice from the first glass and coat it with the absinthe or Herbsaint, then discard excess. Strain the rye, sugar and bitters mixture from the second glass into the first glass.

Dip lemon peel in drink and twist to release oils into liquid. Rub peel along rim of glass and discard.

COCKTAIL FEATURED in *State of the Union*

8. **State of the Union,** 1948. Despite his cheating, a highly moral woman convinces her political-candidate husband (Tracy) to stay true to his convictions.

9. **Adam's Rib,** 1949. Lawyers, Adam and Amanda, have a marriage based on trust and sharing...until they wind up on opposite sides of a highly publicized case where a distraught wife has tried to shoot her cheating husband...and then the sparks really begin to fly! **BUZZ:** A Raquel Welch fave. **QUOTE:** "For years, women have been ridiculed, pampered, chucked under the chin. I ask you, on behalf of us all, be fair to the fair sex." — Amanda Bonner

10. **The African Queen,** 1951. Bogie and Hepburn chew up the scenery as an ol' rummy riverboat captain and a straight-laced missionary lady who take on the Germans in WWI Africa. Bogart won Best Actor.

11. **Pat and Mike,** 1952. Garson Kanin and Ruth Gordon wrote this screenplay featuring Kate's natural athletic abilities, and her preference for wearing slacks. As an athlete (Hepburn), Pat's fiancé only inhibits her, but Mike (Tracy), the sports promoter, knows a "cherce" piece when he sees one.

12. **The Rainmaker,** 1956. Lizzie, nearly a spinster, doesn't know how to please a man until Starbuck (Burt Lancaster) comes to town and teaches her how to love herself first.

13. **Desk Set,** 1957. Fearful of losing her job, Bunny Watson matches wits with the new company efficiency expert (Spencer Tracy) and finds, despite constant sparring, a certain chemistry has developed between them.

"Nature…is what we are put into this world to rise above."

— Rose (Katharine Hepburn),
The African Queen

Adam's Rib

This Ruth Gordon-Garson Kanin script is one of the most overtly feministic of the Tracy & Hepburn vehicles. It's still a great comedy, but it also explores mid-century differences in perception between men and women. When a distraught wife shoots her philandering husband after following him to his lover's apartment, our stars, a couple of married attorneys who disagree about lots of things, wind up on opposite sides of a very contentious legal gender battle.

Among other things, the Bonners completely disagree about a woman's role as a full partner in the marital relationship. Before Amanda Bonner takes on the controversial Attinger case, "Pinky" (Adam Bonner) makes a brainless comment about the weaker sex, and "Pinkie" (Amanda), fed up with Adam's anachronistic attitude, decides that's the straw that broke the camel's back—the female camel, anyway. Afterward, she takes on the case in earnest and it does not please Adam in the least. He begs her to drop the case, but when begging doesn't work, he threatens to cut her into 12 little pieces and feed her to the jury, which, of course, merely whets Amanda's appetite for seeing that Doris Attinger gets the defense she so justly deserves.

As the case against Doris' cheating and abusive husband heats up, it provides the perfect forum for Amanda's personal cause for equal rights under the law for women. Both Bonners are shocked, however, when public conflict intrudes itself on their personal life...but neither is willing to concede their war of words. Minor skirmishes escalate to all-out war, and no amount of "reason" can force Amanda to back off her stance on the inequity of the social standard that treats women differently than men under the law.

"To be loved is very demoralizing."

— Katharine Hepburn

When Adam admits he's *really* sore at Amanda, and even ashamed of her, out come tears from the "fair sex," only proving his point. And when Adam gives Amanda "a little slap," that she considers "typical male brutality," it only proves hers. So Amanda brings out the big guns in court—competent and successful professional women—and declares "the court must be fair to the fair sex!" But as far as Adam is concerned, "Women's Rights" is a dimwitted cause and Amanda's concern with it shows disrespect for him and the law. In conclusion in court, Amanda raises the question of consideration for a woman protecting her home "just like a man" and Adam, stammering his disapproval of such nonsense, loses the case. In retaliation, Adam brings out a gun of his own... at home.

Because this film was made in 1949, Amanda is ultimately forced to feel guilty for taking on such a powerful male myth, and in order to hang onto her marriage, must capitulate, stop competing with Adam, and slip back into her "more appropriate" role as designated peacekeeper. Despite the ending, the repartee is sharp, and the battle between Hepburn and Tracy is fast, fun and irreverent... who, by the way, are perfect as the 1940s funniest battling couple.

BUZZ: Judy Holliday created the role of Billie Dawn in *Born Yesterday* on Broadway. Hepburn was such a fan of Holliday's that among other things, she encouraged *Adam's Rib* director, George Cukor, to let the camera linger on Holliday (Doris Attinger) in her court room scenes to help persuade the studio to give her the role of Billie Dawn on screen. Holliday got the part.

"If you obey all the rules you miss all the fun."

— Katharine Hepburn

14. **The Lion in Winter,** 1968. The message or the messenger? Hollywood has given us many versions of history from The Alamo to Robin Hood. *The Lion in Winter* is probably no exception to this, but the fierce and still tender scene where Eleanor says: "Oh, my piglets we are the origins of war..." is a message we still respond to. Although other female stars of that day could have spoken those words, they could never have delivered them to us. Kate Hepburn's heart seems to shine through that scripted monologue, and that is why we love her films; we believe her voice. **– Guest Reviewer, Mary Lou McAuley.**

15. Kate Hepburn on *The Dick Cavett Show,* September 14, 1973, TCM.

16. Katharine Hepburn: All About Me, 1993, TV documentary (For more, read Kate's bio, "Me: Stories of My Life," on which this film is based.) Hosted and narrated by Katharine Hepburn. **QUOTE:** "Let's face it, it's how you live that counts...Listen to the song of life."

17. Katharine Hepburn: On Her Own Terms, 1996, A&E *Biography* episode narrated by Harry Smith.

"You know, a dame with a rod is like a guy with a knitting needle."

— Jack (Steve Brodie), *Out of the Past*

LIST IV – Love Is a Battlefield

"Fighting is essentially a masculine idea; a woman's
weapon is her tongue."
—Hermione Gingold

Top "Love Is a Battlefield" Movies

* *The Taming of the Shrew, 1929 & 1967*

* *McLintock!, 1963*

* *Who's Afraid of Virginia Woolf?, 1966*

* *Swept Away, 1974*

* *Stepford Wives, 1975*

* *Much Ado About Nothing, 1993*

* *Married Life, 2007*

"Politics doesn't make strange bedfellows—marriage does."

— Groucho Marx

Love Is a Battlefield MOVIE LIST

1. **The Taming of the Shrew,** 1929 & 1967.
Mary Pickford & Douglas Fairbanks, Elizabeth Taylor &
Richard Burton in Shakespeare's battle-of-the-sexes
classic.

2. The Nagger at Breakfast, 1930 (Short).
Married couple's battle of words over breakfast.

3. Cleopatra, 1934. DeMille's lush Cleo with Claudette
Colbert—a powerful woman at her most beguiling.

4. Murder on the Blackboard, 1934. Edna May
Oliver and James Gleason spar over murder from both
sides of the gender divide in one of three such pairings.

5. Bride of Frankenstein, 1935. Elsa Lanchester.
What with those white streaks of hair emanating like
bolts of electricity from her temples, James Whale's
campy *tour de horror* features one of the most iconic
bridezillas ever put on film.

6. Annie Oakley, 1935. A pistol packin' mama's
(Barbara Stanwyck) professional rivalry gets in the way
of her love life.

7. Wife vs. Secretary, 1936. Myrna Loy & Clark
Gable are married, and Jimmy Stewart is sweet on Jean
Harlow…but will Harlow and Gable's working closely
together spoil everything?

8. The Moon's Our Home, 1936. Margaret
Sullavan & Henry Fonda are a fightin' and a lovin'!
BUZZ: A Bill Murray fave.

9. Dodsworth, 1936. Walter Huston & Ruth Chatterton
play a couple on their second honeymoon in Europe
who grow quickly apart when the Mrs. seeks her lost
youth in vain, and becomes frivolously fashionable.

"Men say they love independence in a woman, but they don't waste a second demolishing it brick by brick."

— Candice Bergen

The Taming of the Shrew

No matter whether 'tis a blow to the ego or a blinding ray of hope, Shakespeare has the ability to capture a single soul-changing moment and sculpt it into an entire play. Although many are one-note dramas, every character and every line are so full of meaning, they are often perfect representations of one uniquely authentic human condition Shakespeare plucked from his universe and constructed with poetic precision. Many of his words and phrases conjure up deep emotion, impacting every fiber of our being still to this day.

Then Zeffirelli came along and improved on Shakespeare's poetic precision. Zef's gorgeous Shakespearean-eyecandy movies have a very unique view—they're florid, bold, vulgar, colorful, and filled with bigger-than-life moments. Zeffirelli, much like Shakespeare, manages to inject every possible emotional response at his disposal into a stream of thought passing through a character's mind in a moment of extreme duress, such as a surge of joy or a stab to the heart, in cinematic ways and within cinematic limits.

Zef is truly a master in this field, and he excelled in one of the top battle-of-the-sexes movies ever made—*The Taming of the Shrew* with Richard Burton and Elizabeth Taylor. With so many words to play with, Zeffirelli was forced to pace the master—bold stroke for bold stroke, bridging age with youth and death with sex, and adding color, music and eye-popping production values at just the right moments—all the while keeping the film in check for modern audiences.

The sexual politics rings with authenticity. It hums with old wives' tales and age-old beliefs about gender roles. It speaks to the accusations and private confessions men make about

"Women are like cats—invariably, they land on their feet."

— Sherlock Holmes (Nicol Williamson), *The Seven-Per-Cent Solution* women, and women about men. And the controversy revolves around Kate, who blows everyone's mind by believing women are not inferior beings. Constantly swimming upstream against the beliefs of her day, she exhausts her patience trying to teach her egalitarian insights to the ignorant masses. Like cutting water with scissors, Kate struggles to gain ground, and is not only cut off from love, but also becomes highly embittered by her lack of success. As the story goes, all who know her, fear her.

Pimped out by her father and sister for reasons of their own, the unmarriageable Kate is to be put in her "proper place" by the intrepid, hired-hand Petruchio who sets out to tame her. Supposedly, he dost save her from herself, and eventually, she dost find kindness and integrity in this swaggering, reckless husband of hers! Meanwhile Petruchio discovers a passionate and gentle heart buried beneath Kate's rebellious, man-eating exterior. So finally, the hatchet is buried with a wink and a nod, and though the end of this merry romp is a happy one, we who live in the real world can only wish complicated battles could be so easily resolved by conciliatory moments of gender surrender.

TAGLINE for *The Taming of the Shrew*: "In the war between the sexes, there always comes a time for unconditional surrender."

BUZZ: Word has it, filming 1929's *The Taming of the Shrew* was rough on stars Mary Pickford and Douglas Fairbanks. Their marriage was on the rocks and Fairbanks, being a very physical actor, apparently took out some of his frustrations on Pickford. Meanwhile, Pickford not only had trouble with Fairbanks' treatment of her, but also with her grasp of Shakespeare.

"You women are always raising hell about one thing when it's something else you're really sore about."

— G. W. (John Wayne),
McLintock!

10. **Libeled Lady**, 1936. Scheming against the opposite sex is a personal AND professional hallmark of this witty battle between William Powell, Jean Harlow, Spencer Tracy & Myrna Loy.

11. **Shall We Dance**, 1937. Musical star, Linda Keene (Ginger Rogers), is artfully manipulated by the men in her life (Fred Astaire, Edward Everett Horton, Eric Blore, & Jerome Cowan).

12. **Sweethearts**, 1938. MacDonald & Eddy musical fare about unconventional entertainers with very witty dialogue (half of which was written by Dorothy Parker).

13. **The First 100 Years**, 1938. Wife loves her husband, but she's *really* crazy about her career!

14. **Pygmalion**, 1938. Leslie Howard plays iconic Henry Higgins who thinks he knows who women are.

15. **The Women**, 1939. Biting wit about the complexities of men and women, fidelity and friendship, and all the rest. Norma Shearer heads the cast of many women…and *only* women.

16. **Dance, Girl, Dance**, 1940. The first *real* female director, Dorothy Arzner, looks at the life of a woman (Maureen O'Hara) who accomplishes her dream through her own, not a man's, efforts.

17. **The Maltese Falcon**, 1941. Bogie tells Mary Astor straight out—even if you love 'em, you can't let 'em play you for a chump.

18. **Mr. & Mrs. Smith**, 1941. **BUZZ:** Carole Lombard & Robert Montgomery star in Hitchcock's only screwball comedy—*The War of the Roses* from a kinder and gentler era.

19. **Double Indemnity**, 1944. Fred MacMurray meets his match in the wickedly fatale femme, Stanwyck.

"There are two dilemmas that rattle the human skull: How do you hang onto someone who won't stay? And how do you get rid of someone who won't go?"

— Gavin (Danny DeVito),
The War of the Roses

20. **The Big Sleep**, 1946. Bogie shines as Marlowe, the hard-boiled private dick who not only has a real set of ethics, but also the hots for one of his client's two beautiful daughters (Bacall).

21. **It Shouldn't Happen to a Dog**, 1946. First, a *girl* gets Harry Morgan's crime reporter job, and then he has to battle with a beautiful lady cop and her dog over the McGuffin that's going to get him his job back.

22. **Unfaithfully Yours**, 1948. Rex Harrison battles the green-eyed monster while waving his baton around in the air.

23. **A Letter to Three Wives**, 1949. Just as three women board a boat full of children on a day trip, a letter arrives announcing the chic and single Addie Ross has run off with one of their husbands. But it doesn't say which one....

24. **Annie Get Your Gun**, 1950. Betty Hutton & Howard Keel shoot and flirt and fight. **VIZ:** Song, "Anything You Can Do, I Can Do Better" (Irving Berlin).

25. **All About Eve**, 1950. Bette Davis. Everyone wants a piece of Margo Channing…so, it's only natural they all get to feel the sting of her scorn: "Fasten your seatbelts, it's going to be a bumpy night!"

26. **The Marrying Kind**, 1952. Marriage and money can prove to be a big problem in any era.

27. **The Quiet Man**, 1952. John Ford made a film about an Irish lass (Maureen O'Hara) that's as determined and spirited as the man (John Wayne) that fights for her.

28. **Kiss Me Kate**, 1953. "Cole Porter" develops a musical version of *Taming of the Shrew,* where two divorced actors play the parts…both on stage and off.

"The only time a woman really succeeds in changing a man is when he is a baby."

— Natalie Wood

29. **The Moon Is Blue**, 1953. One determined young virgin undergoes some witty arm-twisting in the guise of two aging suitors, William Holden & David Niven.

30. **Carmen Jones**, 1954. Dorothy Dandridge & Harry Belafonte. Fickle femme fatale gets her young army officer into hot water. **BUZZ:** Based on the Bizet opera, *Carmen*.

31. **Phffft!**, 1954. Judy Holliday & Jack Lemmon's marriage sputters and stalls out...but it's not over. **BUZZ:** George Axelrod wrote this and also wrote the screenplay for *Breakfast at Tiffany's*. **QUOTE:** "Some of them [women] are weepers, some of them are talkers. Some of them are screamers. I always like the screamers. They're more of a challenge." — Charlie

32. **Seven Brides for Seven Brothers**, 1954. Jane Powell & Howard Keel, and at least 12 others, sing, dance and fight about the perils of love.

33. **To Catch a Thief**, 1955. Grace Kelly tries her best to ensnare the elusive cat burglar, John Robie (Cary Grant), in this mid-century modern screwball.

34. **Oh, Men! Oh, Women!**, 1957. This doctor-patient relationship explores the hilarity of a woman's need to be dominated by her alpha-male husband.

35. **Designing Woman**, 1957. Lauren Bacall & Gregory Peck battle in Vincente Minnelli's man-vs.-woman, writer-vs.-designer screwy take on marital conflict.

36. **Pillow Talk**, 1959. Rock Hudson, womanizer, hogs the two-party phone line from career girl, Doris Day.

37. **Cash McCall**, 1960. James Garner & Natalie Wood spar over big business, sex and wheeler-dealer lifestyles.

Frank the Spank

INGREDIENTS

2 ounces Stoli Blueberry Vodka
1 1/2 ounces Triple Sec
1 whole, fully hand-squeezed lime

PROCEDURE

Add all ingredients in a shaker with ice. Shake vigorously and strain into a Martini glass.

ORIGINAL COCKTAIL courtesy of Ashland Mixologist, Frank Dalziel.

38. **A Breath of Scandal,** 1960. Sophia Loren & John Gavin are royally and romantically combative *à la* Vienna.

39. **Lover Come Back,** 1961. Rock Hudson & Doris Day are warring advertising agents in this gender farce.

40. **Jules and Jim,** 1962, French. Truffaut's tragic love triangle between two friends and an independent but fickle woman.

41. **McLintock!,** 1963. George Washington McLintock (John Wayne) rescues his town from his snobby wife (Maureen O'Hara) and damn near destroys it!

42. **8 ½,** 1963, Italian. Fellini's whole life as a director has been a minefield of women…off screen and on.

43. **The Pink Panther,** 1963. David Niven, Peter Sellers, and Robert Wagner all worship and manipulate women in very entertaining, cat burglar-type ways. **VIZ:** Henry Mancini composed the iconic theme music.

44. **Cat Ballou,** 1965. Jane Fonda & Lee Marvin. A drunken gunfighter and the wildest gal in the West wreak revenge on Kid Shelleen. Marvin won Oscar.

45. **Who's Afraid of Virginia Woolf?,** 1966. Taylor and Burton in "The" Gender Battle Royale.

46. **Two for the Road,** 1967. Audrey Hepburn & Albert Finney characterize love and marriage through several decades and phases of wedded-ness. **VIZ:** Another glorious score by Mancini—supposedly one of his own favorites.

47. **The Thomas Crown Affair,** 1968 & 1999. Steve McQueen & Faye Dunaway; Pierce Brosnan & Renee Russo. A superb battle of upper-crust male/female wits and libidos.

[After his wife throws a cake at his head:]

"You should not drink and bake!"

— Kaminsky (Arnold Schwarzenegger),
Raw Deal

48. **John and Mary**, 1969. Contentious love and a lot of gender one-upmanship make this one-night stand a shoo-in for battle status.

49. **Carnal Knowledge**, 1971. Jack Nicholson & Art Garfunkel play self-indulgent men inflicting their sexual delusions on female partners Candice Bergen & Ann-Margret. Too much information!

50. **Divorce His - Divorce Hers**, 1973. The Burtons each give their own distinct view of the disintegration of a marriage.

51. **A Doll's House**, 1973. Claire Bloom. A woman realizes her marriage is a sham—trivialized by an undeserving husband and fantasies about her wifely duties—and leaves.

52. **Alice Doesn't Live Here Anymore**, 1974. Ellen Burstyn won Best Actress for her role as a widow who has to make a new life for her and her son. One of Scorsese's best.

53. **Swept Away,** 1974, Italian. Lina Wertmüller, first of only four women to ever be nominated for a director Oscar, had a uniquely Italian POV when it came to gender issues. In this Battle Royale classic, she mixed together class-status reversal, a deserted island, and a really great love-hate relationship. Giancarlo Giannini still delivers to this day.

54. **Black Moon**, 1975, French. This Louis Malle battle-of-the-sexes fantasy mixes both a unicorn and the wholesale killing of women in an all-out war.

55. **The Stepford Wives,** 1975. Katharine Ross & Paula Prentiss. Men prefer robotic wives geared toward sex and domestic servitude to real women.

"Women are always under the impression that men love them more than they really do."

— Charlie (Liev Schreiber),
The Painted Veil

Swept Away

When Lady Lanzetti...Raffaella..."rich bitch," "industrialist whore," is stranded on a desert island with Gennarino Carunchio, a "sloppy southerner" and Sicilian deck hand from her yacht, the tables get heavily turned in this hard-core battle-of-the-sexes fable directed by Lina Wertmüller. Used to constant pampering while simultaneously haranguing and insulting anyone she perceives as her subordinate, Lady Lanzetti is in for a rude awakening when the anti-industrialist and deeply committed Communist Gennarino quickly tires of her incessant abuse.

With Lady Lanzetti's mouth going non-stop, I was hoping for a quick end to the film...with Gennarino maybe tossing her off a cliff. Unfortunately, now that he has the upper hand, he decides to humble her with his own brand of abuse and steady stream of political drivel. It soon—way too soon—turns into a sexual Lord-and-Master play, reducing Miss High-and-Mighty to a bowl of quivering feminine jelly who feels "swept away" by her unusual destiny and, despite their differences and her beliefs, is quickly enslaved by "love."

Even Gennarino thinks she's crazy, but that doesn't keep him from taking full advantage of her and his new-found power over her. Despite lots of screwing and numerous beatings, Her Ladyship continues to be besotted with her new benefactor; yet grounded in reality as only a peasant can be, he's well aware that the tables would turn again quickly enough if they hadn't been shipwrecked together. And, when a yacht shows up on the horizon, Raffaella tries to convince Gennarino to let it go on by, but instead, he hails it to prove she now loves him more than anything else in the world.

"You shoot off a guy's head with his pants down, believe me, Texas ain't the place you want to get caught."

— Louise (Susan Sarandon), *Thelma & Louise*

Silly guy. As she says, "The world's built in such a cruel way, it could change us again." And despite their new-found trust and his grand gesture, so it does. Giancarlo Giannini plays the Sicilian peasant, and Mariangela Melato plays the lady industrialist in this thought-provoking, gender-based role reversal romp.

BUZZ: Kathryn Bigelow may be the only female director to win an Oscar for Best Director (*The Hurt Locker*, 2008*)*, but Lina Wertmüller was the first woman to ever be nominated for Best Director. Her nomination for her 1975 film, *Seven Beauties,* stood for nearly 20 years until Jane Campion came along with 1993's *The Piano*. Sofia Coppola is the 4th female Oscar-nominated director for her 2003 film, *Lost in Translation.*

VIZ: The beautiful blues of the sea and water around the island are matched only by the big beautiful blue eyes of the two main actors.

"The war between the sexes is over. We won the second women started doing pole dancing for exercise."

— Jacob (Ryan Gosling),
Crazy, *Stupid Love*

56. **The Goodbye Girl,** 1977. Marsha Mason & Richard Dreyfuss play wonderfully combative, unintentional NYC roommates. Both were nominated and Dreyfuss won Best Actor.

57. **A Wedding,** 1978. Carol Burnett. Robert Altman's 70s-style comedy of manners is a chaos of gender and social issues.

58. **Kramer vs. Kramer,** 1979. Dustin Hoffman & Meryl Streep go head-to-head over custody of their son. **BUZZ:** Won five Oscars: Best Actor, Best Supporting Actress, Best Director, Best Picture and Writing.

59. **Willie & Phil,** 1980. 1980s version of *Jules and Jim* stars an earthy and authentic Margot Kidder. **VIZ:** This film has some of the greatest NYC-centric music since Gershwin...Claude Bolling.

60. **The World According to Garp,** 1982. Robin Williams, Glenn Close & John Lithgow. This is the story of Garp and his unconventional family, including his famous feminist mother.

61. **Hasta Cierto Punto,** 1983, Spanish. Filmmaker has big problems with machismo and a liberated lady.

62. **Romancing the Stone,** 1984. Kathleen Turner & Michael Douglas flirt and fight their way through Colombian jungles of danger, mudslides and crocodile-infested waters.

63. **The Good Father,** 1985. When feminism robs a man of his family, an embittered friend decides to help him get even.

64. **The Big Easy,** 1986. Dennis Quaid & Ellen Barkin are on FIRE in this New Orleans homicidal love story!

"Men are such c*ck suckers aren't they?
You don't have to answer that. It's true."

— Daryl Van Horn, *The Witches of Eastwick*

65. **The Witches of Eastwick**, 1987. Jack Nicholson plays the *ultimate* womanizer. **QUOTE #1:** "So whaddya think? Women…a mistake…or DID HE DO IT TO US ON PURPOSE?" — Daryl (Jack) **QUOTE #2:** "I don't think that men are the answer to everything." — Alexandra (Cher)

66. **True Love**, 1989. Bronx Italian gender issues. **QUOTE:** "She tells me stuff, and she says it's important…and I don't even know what the f*ck she's talking about!" — Mikey, the Groom

67. **Dogfight**, 1991. The Marine with the ugliest date wins a prize.

68. **He Said, She Said**, 1991. Kevin Bacon and Elizabeth Perkins share opposing viewpoints both on their TV show and at home.

69. **Aladdin**, 1992 (Animated). Feisty Princess Jasmine holds out for love. **QUOTE:** "How dare you? All of you! Standing around deciding my future. I am not a prize to be won!" — Princess Jasmine

70. **Groundhog Day**, 1993. Bill Murray & Andie MacDowell. Phil Connors is the arrogant and insufferable jerk all women try to avoid…until he *finally* gets it right, that is.

71. **Paper Hearts**, 1993 (AKA *Cheatin' Hearts*). Sally Kirkland, James Brolin, Kris Kristofferson. Jenny 's about to lose her ancestral home to the bank when her no-good husband comes back to town. **VIZ:** Music by Michael Martin Murphey (of "Wildfire" fame).

72. **Much Ado About Nothing,** 1993. Emma Thompson & Kenneth Branagh play Shakespeare's Beatrice and Benedick, a marriage-phobic couple engaged in a "merry war" of wits, who're tricked into loving one another.

"Woman was born to serve man, not the other way around!"

— Gennarino (Giancarlo Giannini),
Swept Away

73. **Sexual Intent,** 1994. Con man loves to con women, then confess all to his therapist.

74. **True Lies,** 1994. The embattled "Ahnuld" rescues his clever but combative wife (Jamie Lee Curtis), his daughter, *and* his country!

75. **Disclosure,** 1994. Michael Douglas gets sexually harassed by his boss, Demi Moore, and doesn't like it.

76. **Dolores Claiborne,** 1995. Kathy Bates & Jennifer Jason Leigh, mother and daughter, fight separately for survival. **QUOTE:** "Sometimes being a bitch is the only thing a woman has to hold onto." — Selena

77. **Headlong,** 1996. A 13-minute short. It gets hostile.

78. **The First Wives Club,** 1996. Goldie Hawn, Diane Keaton, Bette Midler & Sarah Jessica Parker. Thrown over for newer models, three divorced friends seek revenge on their callous ex-husbands.

79. **Your Friends & Neighbors,** 1998. This is enough to put you off *all* relationships…with either men OR women!

80. **Miss Julie,** 1999. Saffron Burrows is a rich woman of the 1890s who unfortunately likes to argue class and sexual politics.

81. **Marine Life,** 2000. Cybill Shepherd stars as a middle-aged lounge singer who has trouble with men.

82. **We Married Margo,** 2000. Based on a true story, two men, once married to the same woman, become roomies.

83. **What Women Want,** 2000. Mel Gibson listens in on chick thoughts, then uses them for his own gain.

84. **Amy's O,** 2001. Liberated lady author meets chauvinist shock jock and sexual sparks fly.

"No one will ever win the battle of the sexes; there's too much fraternizing with the enemy."

— Henry A. Kissinger

85. **Roger Dodger,** 2002. Cynical, womanizing uncle teaches his 16-year old nephew how to manipulate women for sex.

86. **Chicago,** 2002. Catherine Zeta-Jones, Renée Zellweger, Queen Latifah, John C. Reilly & Richard Gere. No matter the singing and dancing and beautiful ladies, this is about hard-edged women who murder their no-good men.

87. **All the Real Girls,** 2003. Love between a good girl and a player—just conquest or more?

88. **Deliver Us from Eva,** 2003. Gabrielle Union and LL Cool J star in an updated *The Taming of the Shrew.*

89. **Pride and Prejudice,** 2003. Look for "The Pink Bible: How to Bring Your Man to His Knees."

90. **Closer,** 2004. Two couples—four romantically insecure people—locked in sexual warfare to the death of love. Beautiful, but brutal. **VIZ:** Haunting song, "The Blower's Daughter" ("I Can't Take My Eyes Off of You") at the end.

91. **A Good Woman,** 2004. Scarlett Johansson & Helen Hunt. The scandalous Mrs. Erlynne saves an inexperienced young woman from her own scandal. **QUOTE #1:** "Every man is born truthful and every man dies a liar." — Contessa Lucchino **QUOTE #2:** Dumby: "Women inspire us to do great things." Cecil: "Then somehow prevent us from doing any of them."

92. **…And They Lived Happily Ever After,** 2004, French. Burning questions about love, freedom and fidelity bother three married men.

93. **Laws of Attraction,** 2004. When two highly competitive divorce attorneys marry, their competitive spirit really kicks in.

"I love you." — Ronny (Nick Cage)

[She slaps him…twice.]

"Snap out of it!" — Loretta (Cher),
Moonstruck

94. Conversations with Other Women, 2005.
Helena Bonham Carter & Aaron Eckhart meet at a
wedding and spend the night together, sharing
memories and regrets from the past.

95. The Painted Veil, 2006. Edward Norton & Naomi
Watts produce and star in this lush version of W.
Somerset Maugham's riff between an English doctor
and his wife played out in rural China.

96. I Think I Love My Wife, 2007. Chris Rock is
confronted head-on by the heady possibilities of lust
outside of marriage.

97. **Married Life,** 2007. Patricia Clarkson, Chris
Cooper & Pierce Brosnan. Love and marriage can be
quite complicated, indeed.

98. Ice Age 3, 2009 (Animated). Manny & Ellie are
having a baby, but there are a lot of "guy things" going
on too. **QUOTE:** Manny: "Guys don't talk to guys about
guy problems. They just...punch each other on the
shoulder." Ellie: "That's stupid!" Manny: "To a girl....
To a guy, that's like six months of therapy!"

99. He's Just Not That Into You, 2009. Jennifer
Aniston, Drew Barrymore, Jennifer Connelly, Scarlett
Johansson and the men in their lives try to "read" each
other when it comes to romantic intention.

"If you know what women want, you can rule!"

— Dr. J.M. Perkins (Bette Midler), *What Women Want*

LIST V – Girls Just Want to Have Fun

"I've been undressed by kings, and I've seen some things that a woman ain't s'posed to see..."
— *I've Never Been to Me,* lyrics rewritten by Ron Miller for Charlene and performed in *The Adventures of Priscilla, Queen of the Desert*

Top "Girls Just Want to Have Fun" Movies

* **My Man Godfrey,** *1936*

* ***Bringing Up Baby, 1938***

* ***The Lady Eve, 1941***

* ***Some Like It Hot, 1959***

* ***Breakfast at Tiffany's, 1961***

* ***A League of Their Own, 1992***

* ***Down with Love, 2003***

"Oh-ho-ho! If we could only live without men!"

— Catherine the Great (Marlene Dietrich), *The Scarlet Empress*

Girls Just Want to Have Fun MOVIE LIST

1. **Bombshell**, 1933. Jean Harlow rocks Hollywood as "A glamorous film star [who] rebels against the studio, her pushy press agent and a family of hangers-on." [TCM Brief Synopsis]

2. **She Done Him Wrong**, 1933. Mae West & Cary Grant. **QUOTE:** "Why don't you come up some time and see me?" — Lady Lou

3. **It Happened One Night**, 1934. The incomparable Frank Capra directed Claudette Colbert & Clark Gable in this hot-blooded-but-funny belligerency of the sexes in the first (ever) film to win the movie grand slam—all five top Oscars.

4. **Merry Wives of Reno**, 1934. Marital spats, insults, cheating and broken crockery all lead to the battle of the divorce court.

5. **My Man Godfrey,** 1936. A "forgotten man" (William Powell) of the Depression wins the heart of a rich ditz (Carole Lombard) in this classic screwball.

6. **Nothing Sacred**, 1937. A cynical reporter (Fredric March) and an illness-feigning female (Carole Lombard) have a lot of illicit fun together in New York City. **BUZZ:** The first screwball comedy shot in Technicolor.

7. **Double Wedding**, 1937. It's complicated—there are two couples, one of which is the incomparable Myrna Loy & William Powell. No Asta.

8. **Bringing Up Baby,** 1938. Eccentric relationships flourish in this series of adventures with a leopard named "Baby." Another great Kate Hepburn vehicle. Cary Grant ain't bad either.

"Marriage is a great institution, but I'm not ready for an institution."

— Mae West

9. **Yes, My Darling Daughter**, 1939. Ellen & Doug have gone off together…alone…and premarital sex is on everyone's mind.

10. **Ninotchka**, 1939. Garbo laughs! And spars wittily with a Parisian playboy (Melvyn Douglas).

11. **My Favorite Wife**, 1940. Irene Dunne, Cary Grant & Randolph Scott play the shipwrecked wife (given up for dead), the newly re-married husband, and the man the shipwrecked wife spent seven years with, alone, on a deserted island.

12. **She Couldn't Say No**, 1940. Eve Arden. Lawyers butt heads then fall into each other's arms.

13. **The Lady Eve,** 1941. Barbara Stanwyck has a lot of fun with a deck of cards and Henry Fonda. **QUOTE #1:** "They say a moonlit deck is a woman's business office." — Jean **QUOTE #2:** "I need him like the ax needs the turkey." — Jean

14. **Sullivan's Travels**, 1941. Joel McCrea banters mightily with Veronica Lake in a Preston Sturges classic about a goofy filmmaker who hits the road to learn about "real" life during the Depression. **BUZZ:** The title of John Sullivan's serious film about poverty he wants to make? *Oh Brother, Where Art Thou?*

15. **The Bride Came C.O.D.**, 1941. Bette Davis & James Cagney star…and the sparks really fly between these two!

16. **Love Crazy**, 1941. The mister (Powell) gets himself into big trouble with the missus (Loy) and resorts to trickery to keep from getting divorced.

17. **The Palm Beach Story**, 1942. Claudette Colbert & Joel McCrea star in another great Preston Sturges story where she divorces her husband to marry a millionaire…so she can help out her ex-hubby.

"I think men who have a pierced ear are better prepared for marriage. They've experienced pain and bought jewelry."

— Rita Rudner

The Lady Eve

This is Preston Sturges' saucy tale of a lady card shark, Jean, who targets a rich beer magnate's son and fleeces him on a cruise aboard the SS Southern Queen as he's returning home after years of living the simple life of an Amazon Rain Forest snake expert. Jean's "father," Harry, per their agreement, tries to take Charles Pike's money at every opportunity, but when Jean falls for "Hopsy," she tries conversely to protect her new beau.

Simultaneously, Hopsy also develops a kind of befuddled appreciation for Jean ("You have the strangest way of bumping a man down and then bumping him back up again."), and he becomes bewitched, bothered and bewildered—besotted, even. But not for long. You see, if Harry has anything to say about it, Hopsy's being set up for the slaughter.

And so, Jean and Hopsy's idyllic days on the boat are numbered. Hopsy's cranky male nanny, Muggsy, who has a great "manure detector," is trying to counteract Jean's attempts to keep Hopsy cockeyed on perfume, and Harry keeps trying to take Hopsy to the cleaners with a few "friendly" side bets.

Despite everything, however, Jean is moved to jump into a relationship with Hopsy with both feet, and that she does. Although Jean never lies to Hopsy, when he's tipped to the fact that she and Harry are "adventurers," he's stung by his misplaced infatuation with Jean, and no amount of assurances on Jean's part that she intended to tell him the whole truth before they were married will mollify him. Humiliated, he scorns her; outraged at being rejected by a sucker, she vows to get even. Then the *REAL* fun begins.

"Personally, I think if a woman hasn't met the right man by the time she's 24, she may be lucky."

— Deborah Kerr

Jean has an "uncle," played brilliantly by Eric Blore, who provides her the opportunity to visit him in Bridgeport, Connecticut, where it so happens, the Pike family lives, and Jean decides to introduce herself to the unsuspecting family as the Lady Eve from England. Now the dialogue, sharp as a straight razor after the strap, becomes epic Battle-of-the-Sexes material. In good, traditional Shakespearean fashion, there's misdirection, misidentification, the servants are pitted against the master, the knowing against the witless, and of course, the predatory female against the gullible male.

The Lady Eve wins, of course, and pulls off a second coup, winning Charlie Pike's heart yet again. Now the flirting and affections, lovemaking and bickering begin anew, and as obstacles are cleared from the bridal path of these two squabblers, Jean proves that she is "positively the same dame" she always was—the one that was meant for him...Hopsy. Ain't love grand? It's just the way any good disagreement should go between oddballs...er...lovers.

VIZ: Two scenes near the beginning of the movie are hilarious one-of-a-kind Sturges creations: In the first, Jean tracks Hopsy's uneasy seduction by boat hopefuls in her compact mirror, then winds up tripping him. And in the second, she takes Hopsy to her cabin to pick out new evening shoes, and winds up intoxicating him with her perfume and some straight talk about seduction that makes him putty in her hands.

Manhattan

Rye whiskey, the original American whiskey used in a Manhattan, fell out of favor during Prohibition. The "other" American whiskey—bourbon—then became the Manhattan whiskey of choice...unless, of course, you prefer Canadian whiskey. It's subjective. After all, all Sugar needed in *Some Like It Hot* was whiskey, vermouth, a little ice and a hot water bottle.

INGREDIENTS

3 ounces of good bourbon
2 ounces sweet vermouth
2-6 dashes Angostura Bitters
maraschino liqueur/cherry
orange peel

PROCEDURE

Add bourbon, vermouth and bitters to a shaker with at least 1 cup crushed ice. Shake vigorously until "teeth-shatteringly cold" and a little of the ice has melted into the drink. Strain into a small Martini or cocktail glass. Splash in a drop or two of maraschino liqueur for color and zing. Use a cherry instead, if you're partial. Rub a piece of orange peel on the rim of the glass (then discard) for depth of flavor.

COCKTAIL FEATURED in *Some Like It Hot*

18. **June Bride,** 1948. Two magazine journalists assigned to a wedding story swap a lot of barbed relationship coverage.

19. **Little Women,** 1949. This time Jo's played by June Allyson. Sisters just wanna have fuh-un!

20. **Born Yesterday,** 1950. Judy Holliday, William Holden & Broderick Crawford have fun with knowledge. Holliday won Best Actress.

21. **The Marrying Kind,** 1952. Screenwriters Kanin & Gordon supply a lot of the funny yet ingenious truisms about a highly troubled marriage.

22. **The Lady Says No,** 1952. An independent woman author writes a book warning about the dangers of men.

23. **Francis Joins the WACS,** 1954. Donald O'Connor and his talking mule are assigned to an all-female army base. **BUZZ:** Believe it or not, music by Mancini (uncredited)!

24. **Lady and the Tramp,** 1955 (Animated). Love from a different side of the tracks and fun with spaghetti!

25. **The Seven Year Itch,** 1955. Tom Ewell & Marilyn Monroe. When the wife is away, hubby will play…the fantasy field.

26. **Some Like It Hot,** 1959. Marilyn Monroe rattles Tony Curtis & Jack Lemmon's musical cage in this fabulously funny Billy Wilder film. **BUZZ:** The American Film Institute (AFI) voted this movie #1 Funniest Movie, and #22 Greatest Movie of all time!

27. **Come September,** 1961. Gina Lollobrigida, Sandra Dee, Rock Hudson & Bobby Darin. Never fear, oversexed boys or no, the girls have the upper hand.

"I only like two kinds of men, domestic and imported."

— Mae West

28. **Breakfast at Tiffany's,** 1961. Audrey Hepburn & George Peppard. Holly Golightly definitely likes having fun. **VIZ:** Oscar-winning song, "Moon River" is by Mancini.

29. Annie Hall, 1977. Woody Allen & Diane Keaton. Fun with lobsters and love in the 70s! **BUZZ:** Allen won four of the top five Oscars for this movie, but lost out for Best Actor.

30. Roxanne, 1987. Daryl Hannah & Shelley Duvall have a fire hose full of fun with Steve Martin's schnoz.

31. Bull Durham, 1988. Susan Sarandon teaches two baseball boys what a woman wants…and how to play ball as well.

32. Shirley Valentine, 1989. Pauline Collins & Tom Conti. Wife and mum, Shirley, loses touch with who she is until she takes a fabulous trip to Greece.

33. Frankie and Johnny, 1991. Michelle Pfeiffer & Al Pacino. Can a persistently romantic co-worker really win a woman's heart? Doubtful…except in the movies!

34. Switch, 1991. Ellen Barkin's terrific as the sexist pig who gets shot by a girlfriend and reincarnates as a gorgeous chick.

35. **A League of Their Own,** 1992. Geena Davis, Tom Hanks, Madonna, Rosie O'Donnell & Jon Lovitz. Loosely based on the first female professional baseball league during WWII. **TAGLINE for *A League of Their Own*:** "A woman's place is on home, first, second, and third."

36. Love's Labour's Lost, 2000. Kenneth Branagh directed this delightful Shakespearean 1930s musical romp about four couples who swear off love and the opposite sex.

Margarita

Silver tequila mixes better with fruity flavors than gold, so no need to spend big bucks to get a yummy-tasting Margarita. However, you must use fresh lime juice or it just doesn't have the right kick. If you must have it sweeter, just use a little simple syrup.

INGREDIENTS

1 ½ ounces silver tequila
1 ounce fresh squeezed lime juice
1 ounce Cointreau or Triple Sec
Salt, coarse (optional)
lime wedge for garnish

For a refreshing Pomegranate Margarita, up the tequila to 2 ounces, and add 2 ounces POM juice.

PROCEDURE

Add tequila, Cointreau, and juice(s) to a shaker with a decent amount of cubed ice. Shake vigorously and pour with some of the ice into a large stemmed glass rimmed in salt (if desired). If you like blended margaritas, consider adding frozen lime juice or POM ice cubes, then blending with crushed ice and other ingredients. Garnish with lime wedge on rim of the glass.

COCKTAIL FEATURED in *Miss Pettigrew Lives for a Day*

37. **Two Can Play That Game**, 2001. Vivica A. Fox & Morris Chestnut. A smart business woman employs her "Ten Day Plan" to control her man when he steps out of line.

38. **Bridget Jones's Diary**, 2001. Renée Zellweger, Colin Firth & Hugh Grant frolic through the streets of London in lust with one another.

39. **Down with Love,** 2003. It's a colorful and updated version of *The Lady Says No*-meets-*Pillow Talk* when 60s feminist author, Barbara Novak, writes "Down with Love," asserting women don't need a man to be happy. **VIZ:** Song, "Here's to Love" – She: "I'm an old fashioned and you're the cherry." He: "I've got a thirst that's legendary."

40. **Intolerable Cruelty**, 2003. George Clooney & Catherine Zeta-Jones kick up a highly competitive gender spirit.

41. **Bride & Prejudice**, 2004. Gender differences are more fun in Bollywood, Miss Austen.

42. **Fever Pitch**, 2005. Drew Barrymore & Jimmy Fallon have fun with love and the Boston Red Sox.

43. **Hitch**, 2005. When wooing the opposite sex, Will Smith, Eva Mendes & Kevin James get jiggy with it.

44. **Romance & Cigarettes**, 2005. Susan Sarandon & Kate Winslet vie for James Gandolfini in this irreverent and musical look at love and infidelity.

45. **John Tucker Must Die**, 2006. Betty Thomas directs this smart and funny battle between a young player (Jesse Metcalfe) and three of his girlfriends who use the new girl at school to try and break his heart.

"A bit of lusting after someone does wonders for your skin."

— Elizabeth Hurley

46. **Miss Pettigrew Lives for a Day,** 2008. Amy Adams & Frances McDormand play women at the opposite end of the social…and male…scale in gorgeous 1939 London.

47. **Bread and Tulips,** 2008, Italian. Woman rebels against her dead-end existence, leaving behind an ungrateful husband and children, to find a more inspiring life.

48. **The Ugly Truth,** 2009. Katherine Heigl & Gerard Butler. "Man vs. woman." — MSN.com, 7/31/09 Abby is a systematic, control-freak TV producer who's searching for love with a checklist of 10 attributes for her perfect mate. Mike, an on-air guy, believes in lust, seduction and manipulation, but not love. At the end of the movie, a terrified-of-relationships Mike blurts out to angry Abby, twice, "I love you!" including yelling "Shut UP!" When she realizes the sudden paradigm shift, she says, "You're in love with me. Why?" He responds, "It beats the sh*t out of me, but I am." NO LOGIC!!! Love is SIMPLY how we feel. And that's *The Ugly Truth*. Though I still avoid angry redheads…sometimes….
– Guest Reviewer, Warner Springs Monty Tam.

49. **Love and Other Drugs,** 2010. Jake Gyllenhaal & Anne Hathaway. A smooth-talkin' drug rep meets his match in a free spirit who can more than hold her own with a player like him.

"…where do you find a man—a real man—these days?"
— Lauren Bacall

LIST VI – The Great Conquering Hero

"Being a hero is about the shortest-lived profession
on earth."
— Will Rogers

<u>Top "The Great Conquering Hero" Movies</u>

* *Mr. Smith Goes to Washington, 1939*

* *Shane, 1953*

* *To Kill a Mockingbird, 1962*

* *Superman, 1978*

* *Big, 1988*

* *The Shawshank Redemption, 1994*

* *Gran Torino, 2008*

"I think a hero is an ordinary individual who finds strength to persevere and endure in spite of overwhelming obstacles."

— Christopher Reeve

The Great Conquering Hero MOVIE LIST

CLASSIC HEROES:

1. CHARLIE CHAPLIN – *Charlie, the Hero*, 1919. Wasn't Chaplin in this comedy "hero" short, but shoulda been—he's saved many a cinematic soul.
2. GARY COOPER – *Mr. Deeds Goes to Town*, 1936. Longellow Deeds saves all those broken men (during the Depression) out there who're drowning.
3. CLARK GABLE – *Gone with the Wind*, 1939. Rhett-to-the-rescue saves Scarlett at nearly every juncture. "Fiddle-dee-dee!" — Scarlett
4. JIMMY STEWART – *Mr. Smith Goes to Washington*, 1939. Jefferson Smith saves democracy from itself.
5. JOHN WAYNE – *Stagecoach*, 1939. The Ringo Kid saves fellow travelers from the Indians, and saves Dallas…a working girl with a heart of gold…from herself.
6. HUMPHREY BOGART – *To Have and Have Not*, 1944. Steve whistles up Slim (Lauren Bacall) and saves a fugitive from the Nazis.
7. ALAN LADD – *Shane*, 1953. Shane saves the homesteaders from big cattleman Ryker and his hired gunslinger, but it's little Joey that saves Shane.
8. CARY GRANT – *North by Northwest*, 1959. Roger saves a spy (Eva Marie Saint) from saboteurs, evil-doers and death by airplane.

"Oh, Frank, you're the best, you're the champ, you're the master...!"

— Patricia, *The Stepford Wives*

9. **SEAN CONNERY** – *Dr. No*, 1962. James Bond saves Ursula Andress (in an iconic bikini) and the world from "World domination. The same old dream." –- 007

10. **GREGORY PECK** – *To Kill a Mockingbird,* 1962. Atticus Finch's dignified and compassionate treatment of a poor black defendant saves us all.

11. **SIDNEY POITIER** – *Lilies of the Field*, 1963. While fighting with Mother Maria, Homer Smith saves the faith by building her a chapel out in the middle of the Arizona desert.

12. **PAUL NEWMAN** – *The Sting*, 1973. Henry Gondorff, master of the long con, saves Johnny Hooker's (Robert Redford) neck by helping wreak vengeance on a shrewd but soulless bad guy.

MODERN HEROES:

1. **CHRISTOPHER REEVE** – *Superman,* 1978. Superman at his finest not only saves the day, but also steals Lois Lane's heart.

2. **ROBERT REDFORD** – *The Electric Horseman*, 1979. Sonny saves the beautiful horse, Rising Star, and his own soul.

3. **JOHN TRAVOLTA** – *Urban Cowboy*, 1980. Bud saves Sissy (Debra Winger) from a baaad, bad man.

4. **HARRISON FORD** – *Raiders of the Lost Ark*, 1981. Indiana Jones saves the Ark of the Covenant from the Nazis.

5. **RICHARD GERE** – *An Officer and a Gentleman*, 1982. Zack Mayo saves himself first, and then Paula (Debra Winger) from a dead-end factory life.

"Women have always ruled my life…Women rule the world."

— Jon Bon Jovi, Feb 2006 Interview with *Elle*

6. JEFF BRIDGES – *Starman*, 1984. A gentle alien takes on human form and is saved by Jenny, the widow of the man he recreates. He in turn, saves her, too.

7. TOM CRUISE – *Top Gun*, 1986. Maverick saves Navy flyboys from oblivion, but can't save Goose (Anthony Edwards).

8. MEL GIBSON – *Lethal Weapon*, 1987. Riggs saves his partner's (Danny Glover) daughter but nearly loses his mind.

9. TOM HANKS – *Big,* 1988. Josh preserves for all of us the childlike innocence we lose when we give up childish things.

10. ARNOLD SCHWARZENEGGER – *Total Recall*, 1990. Quaid not only saves the mutants, but also all of Mars! **QUOTE:** (*Quaid's wife as she goes for her gun*) "...you wouldn't hurt me, would you, sweetheart? ...be reasonable. After all, we're married!" (*Quaid as he shoots her in the head*) "Consider that a divorce!"

11. JOHNNY DEPP – *Edward Scissorhands*, 1990. The ultimate outsider, gentle Edward saves us from a life of bitterness and hate we hold for those different from ourselves.

12. DANIEL DAY-LEWIS – *The Last of the Mohicans,* 1992. Hawkeye saves his beloved Cora.

13. TIM ROBBINS – *The Shawshank Redemption,* 1994. Andy saves both Red (Morgan Freeman) and himself with nothing more than hope...and it sets them both free. **BUZZ:** The Rita Hayworth movie the prisoners are watching is *Gilda*.

14. WILL SMITH – *Independence Day*, 1996. Captain Hiller saves the world from alien invasion...with a little help from his friends.

"It's the heart afraid of breaking that never learns to dance."

— Bette Midler (Song, "The Rose")

Big

Big is a pretty straight-forward fairytale about a boy of 13, Josh, and his buddy, Billy, who both long to be grown up. Josh gets his chance one day when he makes a wish to be "big" at a carnival fortune-telling machine called "Zoltar Speaks." The next day, Josh is not only "big"—but he's also Tom Hanks! His mom doesn't know him and he doesn't really recognize himself either. But with the help of Billy and some rather scary adults, Josh learns what it really means to be "big," realizing at a fairly early age that it actually pays to preserve one's precious childhood as long as is humanly possible.

This movie often works well because it so easily evokes the nostalgic, slightly bittersweet nature of what it's like to be a happy, carefree child. The story's flawless. Penny Marshall focused her direction on all the right moments, and Hanks was extraordinary as the "kid" who recognizes life is not only about integrating the important parts of our lives, but also about preserving the childlike qualities in our nature.

Poor Josh faces a lot of battles—ageism, personal rejection, competition in the marketplace, as well as experiencing a little gender friction for the first time—but he stays true to himself and manages to save himself for what he really is…a kid—an innocent, fun-loving 13-year old with a family and friends that love him for who he really is. And in a time when kids grow up too fast and learn too many of the wrong things too soon, Josh is a hero of our age—he's uplifting.

VIZ: "Zoltar Speaks," the 1930 fortune teller machine that hands out fortunes on a card, has got to be one of modern film's all-time best props. Also check out FAO Schwartz piano.

"Well, I may be an outlaw darlin', but you're the one stealing my heart."

— J.D. (Brad Pitt), *Thelma & Louise*

15. BRUCE WILLIS – *The Fifth Element*, 1997. Cab driver, Korben Dallas, saves Leeloo AND the planet. **VIZ:** The city where Korben flies his cab is futuristic fare right out of *Metropolis*, and the four activated elements (Earth, Air, Fire & Water) are awesome!

16. RUSSELL CROWE – *L. A. Confidential*, 1997. Bud White is the kind of 50s cop that hates corruption with a passion and is compelled to save women from the violence of men. **BUZZ:** Nominated for nine Oscars, it won two, including one for Kim Basinger.

17. BEN AFFLECK – *Armageddon*, 1998. A.J. (Hero-in-training) helps save the world, and the beautiful Liv Tyler, from a Texas-sized asteroid.

18. GEORGE CLOONEY – *Out of Sight*, 1998. Career criminal, Jack Foley, saves J.Lo's butt, nearly losing his own.

19. MATT DAMON – *All the Pretty Horses*, 2000. John Grady Cole manages to preserve his good Texas character, save his hide, and engender a whole lot of love for the West.

20. DENZEL WASHINGTON – *Man on Fire*, 2004. At all costs, Creasy saves Pita, the little girl he's hired to keep safe.

21. CLINT EASTWOOD – *Gran Torino*, 2008. Walt Kowalski saves the Hmong neighbor boy's life after trying to kill him himself. **VIZ:** Check out Eastwood's title tune, "Gran Torino," as it plays over the end credits.

22. BRAD PITT – *Moneyball*, 2011. Billy Beane, General Manager, saves the Oakland A's by turning baseball, the game he loves with a passion, on its head.

"Find me a man who's interesting enough
to have dinner with and I'll be happy."

— Lauren Bacall

LIST VII – Sexual Warfare in the 21st Century

"Men and women, women and men. It will never work."
— Erica Jong

Top "Sexual Warfare in the 21st Century" Movies

* *His Girl Friday, 1940*

* *9 to 5, 1980*

* *Tootsie, 1982*

* *Moonstruck, 1987*

* *The War of the Roses, 1989*

* *Volver, 2006*

* *Brief Interviews with Hideous Men, 2009*

Champagne Cocktail

INGREDIENTS

1 sugar cube
2-3 dashes Angostura Bitters
1 ounce cognac
chilled champagne

PROCEDURE

Add sugar cube to the bottom of a dry champagne flute and soak with bitters. Cover sugar cube with cognac, then slowly top with chilled champagne.

There are variations, of course—some do not include cognac at all—but at Rick's Café Américain in Casablanca, cognac and Rick's "finest brandy" frequented the drinking scene, so this punchy version of the Champagne Cocktail is probably closest to what they actually drank in the early 1940s. To quote Rick, "Here's looking at you kid."

COCKTAIL FEATURED in *Casablanca.*

Sexual Warfare in the 21st Century
MOVIE LIST

1. ### The Thin Man, 1934. Powell & Loy. Love is mutual respect, partner equality and a dog named Asta.

2. ### The Awful Truth, 1937. A witty and sophisticated, yet hilarious look at divorce.

3. ### His Girl Friday, 1940. Rosalind Russell & Cary Grant. **BUZZ:** Peter Bogdanovich calls this movie, about an ex-husband and ex-wife editor/reporter team, "the battle of the sexes in the men's room."

4. ### Pride and Prejudice, 1940, 1995 (BBC), & 2005's *Pride & Prejudice.* Lizzie vs. Mr. Darcy (Greer Garson & Laurence Olivier; Jennifer Ehle & Colin Firth; Keira Knightley & Matthew Macfadyen) is a very modern battle of wits.

5. ### Casablanca, 1942. Bogie & Ingrid Bergman. Ilsa has a big effect on the wartime men in her life—all the "usual suspects." **VIZ:** Song, "As Time Goes By." **QUOTE:** "We'll always have Paris." –- Rick

6. ### Shadow of a Doubt, 1943. Hitchcock pits young Charlie (Teresa Wright) against Uncle Charlie (Joseph Cotton) in this terrifying story of a self-serving and unhinged gigolo whose murderous nature is uncovered by his adoring niece.

7. ### Vacation from Marriage, 1945 (AKA *Perfect Strangers*). A couple is separated by three year's time and corrupted by war.

8. ### Arabesque, 1966. Gregory Peck helps sophisticated spy, Sophia Loren, crack a code and save a Middle-Eastern country ruler. **VIZ:** Music by...you guessed it...Mancini!

"It's an extra dividend when you like the girl you're in love with."

— Clark Gable

9. **Funny Girl,** 1968. Fanny Brice (Barbra Streisand) is funny, talented and rich, and her star is rising as fast as her husband's (Omar Sharif) ego and business are falling to pieces.

10. **The Happy Ending,** 1969. Jean Simmons & John Forsythe. Housewife feels cheated and uninspired, so leaves her family behind in order to find herself. **VIZ:** Song, "What Are You Doing the Rest of Your Life?"

11. **Play Misty for Me,** 1971. Clint Eastwood & Jessica Walter. Ooooh…sex, guile and an obsessive, murderous rage! All to really cool jazz. **BUZZ:** Eastwood's directorial debut.

12. **Manhattan,** 1979. Woody Allen, Mariel Hemingway, Diane Keaton, Michael Murphy & Meryl Streep. A Gershwin-laced homage to NYC and modern, neurotic love-relationship battles.

13. **9 to 5,** 1980. Dolly Parton, Jane Fonda, Lily Tomlin & Dabney Coleman. Sexual harassment, inappropriate workplace high jinks, all-out warfare, and the best bouncy movie-title tune *ever* make this film a delight. **BUZZ:** Parton told Morley Safer on *60 Minutes* she composed "9 to 5" on set, on her fingernails. She used her nails as percussion instruments on the record as well.

14. **City of Women,** 1980, Italian. Fellini film follows Marcello Mastroianni while he's trapped in a hotel with all women at a feminist convention.

15. **Basic Instinct,** 1992. Police detective (Michael Douglas) gets too wrapped up in a case with a seductively beautiful and potentially lethal suspect (Sharon Stone).

"I was so cold the other day, I almost got married."

— Shelley Winters

9 to 5

Violet (Lily Tomlin) is the efficient administrative assistant propping up the contemptible Mr. Hart—the boss without a heart, but NOT without a raging libido and soul-sucking ego. Condescending and credit-grabbing when it comes to any female except his secretary, Doralee (Dolly Parton), Hart reserves the right to play "come-hither" games with Doralee in hopes of diving into her lush, exposed cleavage. When Judy (Jane Fonda), the newbie, comes on board, the egalitarian Violet and the forgiving Doralee get together with Judy, Hart's newest target, and commiserate, each sharing detailed fantasies about humiliating and getting even with Hart.

Franklin Hart, it seems, likes to pass himself off as the great white hope to the owner of the company, Mr. Hinkle, always cranking up the pressure on the girls. He belittles Judy, chases Doralee, and steals Violet's ideas while simultaneously passing her over for promotion. Finally, last straws all-'round have the girls drinking at Charlie's and singing the Hart song—"What a rat!" "What a liar!" "What a creep!" The pink ghetto enslaves them, but an old-fashioned pot party liberates them. Their imaginations run wild and suddenly, the words they used in their dreams of vengeance (which makes for a hilarious fantasy sequence) inspire them and, finally, they know what they have to do with that "sexist, egotistical, lying, hypocritical bigot!"—their boss.

After a little Big Game hunting, role reversal and Violet's Snow-White fantasy of revenge, the "real" thing of bringing Hart to his knees becomes imperative. So, Mr. Hart is, shall we say, detained...restrained...shackled and chained, and the company's three muses take over the workings of the company—positively spinning policies galore—all in the name

"Would you condescend to come out here and make my coffee!"

— Husband, *The Nagger at Breakfast*

of the resistive-and-male Mr. Hart, who is FINALLY getting a big dose of his own medicine. Dabney Coleman is the perfect stereotypical misogynist and self-absorbed jerk who doesn't have a clue about women or business or anything but himself, really. It's "The World According to Hart," and his *9 to 5* comeuppance is a sheer delight—especially with these three ladies at the helm.

BUZZ: On June 16, 2007 on the "50 Funniest Women Alive" list, Joy Behar said of Lily Tomlin in *9 to 5*, who's #8 on the list, "She's always got that little pixie gleam in her eye."

VIZ: Loved Violet's pot-party-fueled Disneyana fantasy of eradicating the exasperating Mr. Hart. Disney fans... *Cinderella* Alert!

"If only we could accept that there is no difference between us where human values are concerned. Whatever sex."

— Liv Ullmann

16. **Tootsie,** 1982. Dustin Hoffman & Jessica Lange. Who could be a more devastatingly modern and outspoken woman than a man!

17. **Victor Victoria**, 1982. James Garner & Julie Andrews star in one of the most classic gender-benders ever filmed about a starving female opera singer who pretends to be a man pretending to be a woman. **VIZ:** Music by Mancini.

18. **Mask,** 1985. Cher, Sam Elliott & Eric Stoltz. This is the way complex relationships should be—about life *and* death. **QUOTE:** Rusty to Gar: "Why should you be any different than any man I've known before?"

19. **Broadcast News**, 1987. A smartly scripted romance with the intelligently madcap trio of Albert Brooks, Holly Hunter & William Hurt mixing personal integrity and professional ethics.

20. **Fatal Attraction**, 1987. Michael Douglas, Glenn Close & Anne Archer. Welcome to the world of aggressive, psychopathic females, and very *BA-AD* news for adulterers.

21. **Moonstruck,** 1987. Why do men behave the way they do? And OMG...Cher [the Kate Hepburn of our era]: strong, smart, tall, dark and unflappable. **BUZZ:** She won Best Actress for her role as Loretta Castorini.

22. **Someone to Love**, 1987. Filmmaker Henry Jaglom searches for the answer to why, in this day and age, men and women alike tend to be alone. **BUZZ:** Orson Welles' last film appearance.

23. **Women On the Verge of a Nervous Breakdown**, 1988, Spanish. Everyone wants and needs to be in love, apparently. As it happens, the anguish is an awful lot of work for what you get. **BUZZ:** A Rachael Ray fave, especially with Bloody Marias.

"It is possible that blondes also prefer gentlemen."

— Mamie Van Doren

24. **sex, lies and videotape**, 1989. *Everything's* complicated, and when James Spader shows up with a camera and a penchant for videotaping women, a messy threesome gets even more so.

25. **The War of the Roses,** 1989. Kathleen Turner & Michael Douglas. Danny DeVito's *tour de force* Hatfield-and-McCoy, battle-of-the-sexes divorce to the death!

26. **When Harry Met Sally**…, 1989. Billy Crystal & Meg Ryan start off as sparring partners, and wind up as…friends? **QUOTE:** "What I'm saying is…is that men and women can't be friends because the sex part always gets in the way." — Harry

27. **Thelma & Louise**, 1991. Susan Sarandon & Geena Davis. Girl power at full throttle…across the desert and just a *little* outside the men's comfort zone.

28. **Impromptu**, 1991. Judy Davis & Hugh Grant. The strong, individualistic female novelist, George Sand, pursues the timid-but-smitten composer, Frédéric Chopin.

29. **Husbands and Wives,** 1992. Woody Allen, Mia Farrow, the luminously pained Judy Davis, and one of my all-time faves, Sydney Pollack. Four best friends, two couples, share the numbness and pain that attends a marriage's end.

30. **Strictly Ballroom**, 1992. Competitive ballroom dancing has lots of room for gender nuance…oh, yeah. **QUOTE:** "Where the man goes, the lady must follow…." — Liz

31. **The Ref**, 1994. Denis Leary rolls hilariously with the gender punches when he robs a couple and winds up having to step into the role of marriage counselor.

Aphrodisiac

INGREDIENTS

1 shot Baileys Irish Cream
1 shot Kahlua
½ shot brandy
½ shot vodka
1 shot cream

PROCEDURE

Add all ingredients into a shaker with ice, shake vigorously and pour into a chimney glass. Frothy. Or, pour ingredients over ice in a chimney glass and stir. Smooth.

If you don't do cream, leave it out. It'll be strong, but still delicious. Want something hot? Add the above boozes to a hot cup of coffee and add cream or not. Yum.

ORIGINAL COCKTAIL courtesy of ZetMec [@ZetMec].

The War of the Roses

The Roses, Oliver (Michael Douglas) and Barbara (Kathleen Turner), met at an antiquities auction on Nantucket vying for the same piece—two kids fresh out of college, horny and hopeful for the future. Thereafter, the struggling young lawyer and his new wife share a small, cramped space with two small children and a lot of legal briefs. But, as the Roses' income and social status rise, Oliver's elitist tendencies start to grate on Barbara. He cares desperately about what everyone thinks, so Barbara throws her own unfulfilled longings and all her spare time into finding the perfect house for her dear little family... and one day, much to Oliver's surprise, she finds it.

The house is huge. It has an incredible chandelier in the entryway, and while Oliver works day and night at the firm, Barbara sweats every decision, working to bring the house to a state of finished perfection. Once done, however, Oliver senses a change in Barbara. Irritatingly for Oliver, Barbara seems to have developed a mind of her own. When she takes up making liver pâté at home as a hobby, Oliver insists they hire a live-in so his quality of life doesn't suffer; but in essence, he's pressuring Barbara to revert to the same nurturing, malleable woman he married, whom he fully expects to cheerfully reflect all his tastes and wishes... forever.

As the war heats up, Oliver tosses Barbara's cat aside whenever it crosses his path, and she teases his dog, Benny, unmercifully whenever possible. He denigrates her interest in cooking; she turns on all the kitchen appliances to drown out the sound of his voice. The conflict escalates when Barbara doesn't respond appropriately to Oliver's health scare, and he becomes petulant, proceeding to trot out a number of rules Barbara is expected to abide by. Instead, Barbara fantasizes

"I was always opinionated."

— Kim Novak

constantly about how happy she would be to be free of him, "as if a weight had been lifted."

Stunned, Oliver demands an apology. She counter-demands a divorce. Dumbfounded, he has no clue what her problem is. She "owes" him he yells! She wants to smash his face in! And the war's full on. But the killer is, when they file for divorce, they both want to keep their just-so perfect house. Oliver declares Barbara will never get it because by all rights, it's his. After all her sweat and tears, Barbara now burns with hatred.

And despite a warning from their lawyer, Gavin (Danny DeVito), to Oliver not to live together in the contested house and under the same roof as parties who "share separate lives," they do anyway, hoping to wrestle their wonderful house away from the other one; and soon, the roof itself is in jeopardy.

Finally, after Oliver runs over Barbara's cat, the physical gloves come off. He insults her and pisses in her food in front of her guests. Barbara crushes Oliver's sports car (a Morgan) with her SUV, he burns her kitchen, she breaks his precious Staffordshires, and they start to get ver-rr-y physical! But all hope is lost once Barbara goes past the point of no return and serves Oliver a little Benny pâté on a cracker.

Now, the house is no longer important. In fact, the house is systematically destroyed, piece by piece, chandelier and all, as *The War of the Roses* scorches the earth, taking out everything [SPOILER ALERT!], the Roses included. It's the "shock and awe" battle of all cinematic battles of the sexes.

BUZZ: Danny DeVito directed as well as acted in this one.

VIZ: Barbara wears a stunning black'n'white gown in the Morgan-crushing scene.

"Loretta, I love you…but love don't make things nice—it ruins everything. It breaks your heart."

— Ronny (Nick Cage), *Moonstruck*

32. ## The Adventures of Priscilla, Queen of the Desert, 1994. Terence Stamp, Hugo Weaving & Guy Pearce. Men and women ("all mix up") frolic to the tune of Abba songs and more!

33. ## Talking About Sex, 1994. The book this comedic movie references discusses contemporary sexual hang-ups.

34. ## Before Sunrise, 1995. A young American and a French student meet on a train, then hang out together for one whole day in Vienna. **QUOTE:** "You know, I have this awful paranoid thought that feminism was mostly invented by men so that they could like, fool around a little more." — Celine

35. ## Pocahontas, 1995 (Animated). She not only fights for the man she loves, but for herself and for change.

36. ## Mr. Wrong, 1996. Ellen DeGeneres & Bill Pullman. You never know how soon you may regret finding the perfect partner. (Just how *wrong* could you be, Ellen?!)

37. ## Bound, 1996. Gina Gershon, Jennifer Tilly & Joe Pantoliano. The girls out-wit, out-gun and out-last the boys.

38. ## Different for Girls, 1996. Two school chums reunite to discover one boy's now a girl...but they *STILL* get along great!

39. ## In the Company of Men, 1997. One misogynist and one jerk set out to ruin the life of the most innocent and uncorrupted female they can find.

40. ## Mulan, 1998 (Animated). A brave daughter, disguised as a boy, replaces her father for his mandatory service in the Chinese army. **QUOTE:** "Just because I look like a man doesn't mean I have to smell like one." — Mulan

"I keep waiting to meet a man who has more balls than I do."

— Salma Hayek

41. **The Opposite of Sex**, 1998. Christina Ricci, Martin Donovan & Lisa Kudrow. Dede is a cynical 16-year old sexpot who causes trouble for *everyone*, including her gay half-brother, claiming his boyfriend got her pregnant.

42. **American Beauty**, 1999. Annette Bening & Kevin Spacey. This perfect couple lives in a perfect house in the perfect neighborhood, and their life and gender issues are all causing perfectly depressing chaos. **BUZZ:** Won five Oscars out of eight noms.

43. **The Story of Us**, 1999. Bruce Willis & Michelle Pfeiffer flash back through 15 years of marriage to where it went wrong.

44. **Love & Sex**, 2000. Famke Janssen & Jon Favreau. Two quirky people come together, but then separate, realizing how tough love'n'war can be in the 21st C.

45. **Bandits**, 2001. Bruce Willis, Billy Bob Thornton & Cate Blanchett. Two bank robbers and their beautiful, fun-lovin' and therapeutic moll share the love.

46. **His Secret Life**, 2001, Italian. Sometimes two contradictory relationship realities exist side-by-side, yet, great beauty exists in both.

47. **Mulholland Dr.**, 2001. David Lynch's movie about absurdist-Hollywood sexual politics and other stuff. **VIZ:** The Angelo Badalamenti score and the visceral rendition of "Crying" at Silencio were *magnifico*.

48. **My Wife Is an Actress**, 2001, French. Charlotte Gainsbourg & Yvan Attal. Marriage is a complex dynamic: What if your wife is a successful…and sometimes nude…actress? How much can you take??

49. **Shrek**, 2001 (Animated). Princess Fiona is an outspoken and independent ogre who knows what she wants.

"Assumptions are the termites of relationships."

— Henry Winkler

50. I Am Dina, 2002, Norwegian. Unpredictable tale of ballsy woman who accidentally killed her mother and now dispels her ghosts with music and men.

51. Far from Heaven, 2002. Julianne Moore, Dennis Quaid & Dennis Haysbert play out two doomed relationships in the socially and sexually repressive 50s.

52. Just a Kiss, 2002. The musical chairs of fidelity, starting with "just a kiss," stand to ruin multiple relationships.

53. Unfaithful, 2002. Diane Lane & Richard Gere. How love and self-indulgence can get confused, and what it can cost you.

54. Complicated Women, 2003 (Documentary). Jane Fonda narrates this film about actresses who starred in pre-code movies when women's roles represented them as liberated, and often, equal or superior to men. Astor, Blondell, Colbert, Crawford, Davis, Dietrich, Garbo, Harlow, Hopkins, Lombard, Loy, Rogers, Shearer, Stanwyck, West & Young, and, of course, Hepburn, to name a few.

55. Coyote Beach, 2003. An old-fashioned power struggle breaks out between a smart young couple at the beach.

56. The Shape of Things, 2003. Rachel Weisz, Paul Rudd & Gretchen Mol. New friends and lovers can change us dramatically, for the good and the not-so-good.

57. Yes, 2004. Joan Allen. Love is many things— sometimes edgy, sometimes low-burning embers, sometimes the complete warp and woof of all colors and textures present in our multi-dimensional world.

"My hope is that gays will be running the world, because then there would be no war. Just a greater emphasis on military apparel."

— Roseanne Barr

58. **Before Sunset,** 2004. Julie Delpy & Ethan Hawke. The *Before Sunrise* couple meet again after nine years and discuss the bond they had those many years ago in Vienna. Richard Linklater film.

59. **Stage Beauty,** 2004. Claire Danes & Billy Crudup. An actor whose reputation relies on his expertise playing women on stage has an unusually complex relationship with his female dresser.

60. **The Trouble with Men and Women,** 2005, English. When it comes to the trajectory of relationships, some of us are willing to leap forward, others not so much. **TAGLINE for *The Trouble with Men and Women*:** "Love is like an aspirin, it takes the pain away but the headache always comes back."

61. **Tuya's Marriage,** 2006, Mandarin. Inner Mongolian woman searches for a new husband who will take care of her, her previous—and now disabled—husband, their children and their land.

62. **The Break-Up,** 2006. Jennifer Aniston & Vince Vaughn. Relationships get very complicated when you have to split up the ol' living space and it can't be split... at least, not right away.

63. **Miss Potter,** 2006. Renée Zellweger & Ewan McGregor. This is the story of the strong-willed Beatrix Potter who wrote warm and fuzzy books about Peter Rabbit and then preserved over 4,000 acres of England's beautiful Lake District.

64. **Volver,** 2006, Spanish. Penélope Cruz plays a complex woman-single mother in the midst of conflict: Her vs. her dad, her mom vs. her dad, her vs. Paco, and Paco vs. her daughter. What more can a girl take?

65. **Teeth,** 2007. Boys pressuring a chaste young thing for sex, experience instead a man's worst nightmare.

"Getting married for sex is like buying a 747 for the free peanuts."

— Jeff Foxworthy

66. **Sita Sings the Blues**, 2008 (Animated). Ancient Hindu-Goddess cautionary tale meets modern-day "bad-boy syndrome" set to a soundtrack of classic ballads. It's "a tale of truth, justice and a woman's cry for equal treatment," according to director, Nina Paley.

67. **Revolutionary Road**, 2008. Kate Winslet & Leonardo DiCaprio. Pressure to be normal in the fast-changing 1950s is well conveyed by Director Sam Mendes as to how it affected men and women very differently.

68. **Vicky Cristina Barcelona**, 2008. Women and men, men and women; woman/woman/man, man/man/woman …phew! Modern coupling…and it's all Javier Bardem's fault.

69. **Amelia**, 2009. Hilary Swank. Strong woman and aviatrix, Earhart believes marriage should have "dual controls."

70. **Ghosts of Girlfriends Past**, 2009. Lothario uncle returns from the dead to convince his womanizing nephew he's wrong to use and abuse women.

71. **The Princess and the Frog**, 2009 (Animated). Tiana is a hard-working female entrepreneur who works two jobs to make her dreams of owning a restaurant come true.

72. **A Woman, A Gun and a Noodle Shop**, 2009, Mandarin. Sometimes, whether old world or new, relationships can get quite complicated. **QUOTE:** "Tell Wang he can't bully me any more!" — Wang's wife

73. **It's Complicated**, 2009. Meryl Streep, Alec Baldwin & Steve Martin play an older threesome who all suffer the hilarious slings and arrows of romantic attachment when old relationships raise new issues.

"But you don't understand, Osgood! I'm a man!" — Jerry

"Well, nobody's perfect." — Osgood, *Some Like It Hot*

74. **Brief Interviews with Hideous Men,** 2009. Men reveal their true POV's about their reactions to women in a series of raw yet incisive interviews and vignettes. John Krasinski's promising directorial debut.

75. **Not Easily Broken,** 2009. Morris Chestnut, Taraji P. Henson. Marital crisis in a modern marriage must endure pressure from all sides.

76. **Made in Dagenham,** 2010, English. Women machinists fight workplace discrimination in 1968 Dagenham, England—equal pay for equal work.

77. **Tangled,** 2010 (Animated). Mandy Moore & Zachary Levi. This modern version of Rapunzel, where both the male and female characters—as well as sassy sidekicks—are equally strong and funny, is a classic.

78. **Potiche,** 2010, French. Catherine Deneuve & Gérard Depardieu. A trophy wife takes on a doubtful business world and becomes a new woman—the boss!

79. **Crazy, Stupid Love,** 2011. Emma Stone, Ryan Gosling, Julianne Moore & Steve Carell star in this hilarious examination of what it takes to love somebody and make somebody love you. **BUZZ:** Matt Lauer loved it.

80. **The Source,** 2011, French. A remote, North African village's women withhold sex when the men won't help haul water from the mountain top—a modern Lysistrata about water instead of war.

81. **Think Like a Man,** 2012. Rom-com battle taken from Steve Harvey's book, "Act Like a Lady, Think Like a Man."

"Hollywood! The dream factory. The magic store. Hey! Don't you ever go to the movies?"

— Dom DeLuise, *The Muppet Movie*

A MOVIE LOVER'S DREAM

♫"Hooray for Hollywood!"♫
----- *Hollywood Hotel,* 1937

In 2014, three Movie Lovers, two from the U.S. and one from Australia, will meet for the first time in L.A. to attend the 2014 Turner Classic Movie (TCM) Film Festival.

So, what do these three Movie Lovers have in common other than classic movies? A Twitter account! Bonding online over favorite films, film stars, and the love of a damn fine cocktail…plus a little Art Deco thrown in for good measure…and going to L.A. for the TCM Film Festival becomes a dream come true.

@LouisaJanexxx, @rsimpson3 and *@ZetMec* from Cronulla, Australia, Austin, Texas and Ashland, Oregon plan to take in one of the best and most stylish film festivals taking place on the planet—and in Hollywood no less—including what L. A., Hollywood and the wonderful old movie palaces have to offer!

Randy's "Old-Fashioned" Old Fashioned

INGREDIENTS

¼ oz rich (2-to-1) simple syrup
2 dashes bitters
2 oz rye whiskey
big swath of orange peel
Tovolo ice cube

PROCEDURE

Muddle orange peel in simple syrup with the bitters (Fee Brothers 1864 Whiskey Barrel-Aged Bitters or Angostura). Add whiskey (Randy prefers Rittenhouse 100 rye whiskey).

Stir. Drop one Tovolo ice cube in an old fashioned glass, pour in drink mixture and serve.

ORIGINAL COCKTAIL INTERPRETATION courtesy of Randy Simpson , Austin, Texas [@*rsimpson3*].

COMING SOON

"Hollywood is like Picasso's bathroom."
----- Candice Bergen

The third book in the GOOD MOVIE GUIDE series, *Movies and Making It in Hollywood,* celebrates movies that share stories reflecting the glamour, the glory and the golden ages of Hollywood, such as:

- *Sunset Boulevard*
- *Singin' in the Rain*
- *The Stunt Man*
- *Swingers*
- *Shadow Magic*

Inside *Movies and Making It in Hollywood,* you'll find dozens of Hollywood-related movies (in sub-genres such as "Star Power," "The Dream Machine," and "Tinseltown"), Buzz, Viz, and celeb quotes about the magic…or soullessness…of movie making.

"I have yet to hear a man ask for advice on how to combine marriage and a career."

— Gloria Steinem

ZetMec's *The Good Movie Guide* Series

- *Movies and The Meaning of Life*

- *Movies and The Battle of the Sexes*

- *Movies and Making It In Hollywood…***COMING SOON!**

ta2

INDEX

The Lists:

Featured Movies:

Guest Reviewers:

The Booze:

Guest Mixologists:

"Enemies are so stimulating."

— Katharine Hepburn

NOTES

NOTES

NOTES

CPSIA information can be obtained at www.ICGtesting.com
Printed in the USA
BVOW041632290313

316842BV00001B/3/P